Sis, Get Your Purse In Order

By
Janean C. Armstrong

Sis, Get Your Purse In Order

Blue Café Books *for*
www.carladupont.com
Atlanta, GA
Printed in the USA.
ISBN: 979-8-218-87862-7

Credits
Editorial: Carla DuPont
Cover Design: Garrett Myers

DEDICATION

I dedicate this book to my one and only, beautiful daughter, Kourtney Janae Hawkins. It is my heartfelt wish that the financial struggles which have been a burden on our family lineage come to an end with you. You are not just my daughter, you are the embodiment of my hopes and dreams, the living proof of my dedication and hard work. In you, I see my legacy, a beacon of what is possible when resilience and determination come together.

As you embark on your journey, always remember that you are my biggest and proudest accomplishment. Your potential is limitless, and I have every confidence that you will navigate life with clarity, self-assurance, and an unwavering sense of freedom. Go forth, my love, and embrace the world with boldness. You have the tools to create a life filled with joy, abundance, and fulfillment.

With all my love,

Mama

CONTENTS

Chapter 6
Sis, Don't Leave Them Debt, Leave Them Wealth

Chapter 7
Sis, Put It In Writing – Wills, Trusts, & The Power of Planning

Chapter 8
Sis, Protect Your Peace And Your Purse

Chapter 9
Sis, Don't Just Dream It, Do It

Chapter 10
Sis, Peace Lives In The Plan

Sis, Get Your Purse In Order

Chapter 1
Sis, Stop Playing With Your Bag

The Importance Of Financial
Education, Particularly For Women

I magine this.

You're at lunch with your girlfriends. The mimosas are flowing, the DJ is spinning, and the table looks like a runway for designer bags. Gucci here, Louis there, and a little YSL sprinkled in. Everyone is smiling for selfies...heads tilted just right, filters on lock. Then, the server drops the check.

Suddenly, the laughter fades. One friend is nervously flipping through her wallet, whispering, "I hope this one goes through." Another starts calculating how many days until payday. Somebody else suggests splitting the bill "evenly." One of the girls laughs and agrees, while wincing internally knowing that $25 "difference" is eating up her gas money for the week. And you? You're staring at the numbers, stomach in knots, hoping your rent check doesn't bounce when it clears on Monday.

Sound familiar? Too many of us are out here looking rich yet living broke. Rocking $300 purses with $3 inside. Leasing luxury cars that double as rolling billboards for our financial stress. Shopping for vacations like we're millionaires while our checking account is wheezing for air.

And if brunch wasn't enough, let's talk about another moment we all know too well...when the phone rings and the number on the screen looks suspiciously like a bill collector.

You don't even have to answer to feel the stress. Your heart skips. You mute the ringer. You turn your phone face down like that'll make the problem disappear. Some of us even save the numbers under fake contacts like "Do Not Answer" or "Spam Likely" just so we don't have to look our money in the face.

One of my girlfriends told me she used to answer and put the phone on speaker just to argue. "Sir, I don't know what you expect me to do with negative $27 dollars in my account. Y'all gonna get paid when I get paid." Another friend said she would sit in the car outside of her apartment, scared to go inside because she knew there was a stack of unopened bills waiting on the counter.

This is no way to live. Constantly ducking calls, living in fear of mailboxes and unknown numbers. That's not freedom, that's financial bondage. And it eats at your peace of mind, your sleep, even your confidence.

You know the truth, avoiding those calls doesn't make the debt disappear. If anything, it makes your debt grow with late fees and interest, and damages your credit score. The only way out is through. The only way through is with knowledge and a plan that encourages you to face it head on.

This isn't to shame you. It's about shining a light on the truth: nobody ever taught us how money really works. When you don't know how to do something, you're forced to fake it...until the faking runs out.

Why Financial Education Matters (Especially for Women)

Let me drop a little history on you. Did you know that before 1974, a woman in America couldn't even open a credit card in her own name without a husband or father co-signing? That was right at 50 years ago. Think about that. Some of our mothers were alive when the system legally told women, you can't be trusted with money unless a man is attached to it."

That law didn't change until Congress passed the Equal Credit Opportunity Act. Even then, changing the law didn't instantly change the culture. For generations, women were told to let "the man of the house" handle the money while we handled the groceries, the kids, and the church bake sale.

Now, fast forward to today. We're running businesses, heading boardrooms, and out here securing the bag. However, a lot of us still didn't get the financial education we needed to feel confident with our money. And you can see it in the numbers:

- 37% of women in the U.S. have less than $500 in savings (Nasdaq).
- Black women carry, on average, the highest student loan balances of any group which is around $41,500 (Educational Data Initiative).
- Nearly 80% of women will be solely responsible for their finances at some point in life (through divorce, being single, or outliving a spouse).

These are not just statistics, these are our stories. That's your auntie struggling to retire. That's your cousin dodging calls from Sallie Mae. That's your co-worker whose husband handled everything until he walked out, and now she doesn't even know the password to her online banking account.

The bigger picture is when women lack financial knowledge, it doesn't just hurt us. It hurts our families, our kids, and even our communities. The truth is, women are often the ones managing the household budget, deciding what gets paid, what gets pushed, and how far that dollar stretches. When we're financially strong, the whole house is strong.

Financial education is not about turning you into an economist. It's about giving you confidence. Confidence to say no to debt traps. Confidence to negotiate your salary. Confidence to invest in your future without second-guessing every move.

And let me say this with love: a man is not a financial plan. Even if you've got a partner who "handles everything," you still need to be in the know. When life changes, and it will, you don't want to be left learning money lessons in the middle of a crisis.

Your money education is your armor. It's your power. It's what allows you to live life on your terms instead of letting life happen to you.

Sis, financial education isn't a luxury, it's a survival skill.

Think about the big financial picture. Bills don't stop because you're a woman. The rent doesn't spontaneously get smaller when your job underpays you. The bank doesn't say, "Oh, she's a good person, let's forgive the overdraft fee." And when life hits hard – and it always does – the only thing standing between you and disaster is what you know about your money.

Here's why financial education is especially urgent for women.

- **We live longer.** On average, women outlive men by five years. That means our money has to stretch further in retirement.
- **We earn less.** Black women earn about 64 cents for every dollar a white man makes. That's not just a statistic, it's a reality that means we're starting the race from behind.
- **We step away from work more often.** Whether it's to

raise kids, care for aging parents, or support family, women are more likely to pause careers. That means less money saved, less retirement built.

- **We face more financial headwinds.** From the student loan crisis (where Black women carry the highest average balances) to healthcare costs to divorce, the money math is not set up in our favor.

Let's be honest, for too long, society told women to "let the man handle the money." But sis, what happens when there is no man? When the man leaves? Or the man passes away? If you don't know what's going on with your finances, you are gambling your whole life on somebody else's choices.

Dependence is not a financial strategy.

Janean's Story: Learning Early

I was primarily raised by my father, a dedicated man who worked tirelessly to provide for my brother and me. When I was 11 and my brother was just 7, we made the big move to live with him. Life with Dad was filled with lessons about hard work and determination; however, there was a gap in his knowledge when it came to managing money and credit.

The only taste of credit I got growing up was the occasional small charge at a local drug store, basically just store credit. This limited exposure left me completely unprepared for the financial world that awaited me as an adult. As I got ready for college, it became quickly apparent that I knew nothing about important topics like credit scores or how to use a credit card responsibly. It was shocking to see that no one—neither my parents nor my high school teachers—ever talked about financial literacy. The closest we got to a money lesson was hearing that we didn't have any.

When I began college, I was excited to dive into new experiences. In my eagerness, I fell for the lure of credit card offers, tempted by free t-shirts and book bags. Before I knew it, I had signed up for ten different credit cards, each with its own balance and due date. I didn't make a single payment, thinking it was no big deal. I was young and naive, blissfully unaware of the storm brewing on the horizon.

Then came graduation day. I was jolted into reality with a credit score of just 400. That number was a harsh wake-up call, making it nearly impossible for me to rent an apartment in my name. The weight of my financial ignorance felt unbearable. I had learned a tough lesson the hard way. It took me ten grueling years to finally sort out my finances, navigating the ups and downs of credit repair and picking up crucial lessons about money management along the way. Looking back, I can see just how vital it is to teach financial literacy to young people so they won't have to face the struggles I did.

Breaking It Down: Practical Steps To Get Educated

Let's get into the "how," because knowledge without action is just trivia.

Step 1: Get real about where you are...

Stop guessing about your money. Write it down.

- What's your monthly income (after taxes)?
- What are your monthly expenses? Be honest. Netflix, DoorDash, hair appointments, nails, Amazon...that all counts.
- Subtract expenses from income. What's left? Positive or negative?

Facing the numbers might sting, but sis, you can't fix what you won't face.

Step 2: Learn one new thing every week.

Financial education doesn't mean enrolling in an MBA program, it means choosing to learn routinely.

- Follow one credible financial voice online (not your cousin selling Forex scams).
- Read one article, one blog, or listen to one podcast about money each week.
- Keep a "money journal." Write down what you learned in your own words. Seeing it in black and white makes it stick.

Step 3: Talk about money out loud.

We'll talk about everything else like our relationships, kids, trips we plan to take, but money is always taboo. Not anymore. Not for you.

With friends: Instead of only talking about shoes or vacations, try weaving money talk into the mix.

- "What's your credit score goal this year?"
- "Anybody started investing yet?"
- "Y'all, my credit score just hit 700! I didn't even know how much paying off one small card could boost it."
- "Ok, who's using a budgeting app? I'm trying to stop these late-night Amazon shopping sprees."
- "We're always talking about traveling...what if we each saved $50 a month in a trip fund? That way when it's time, nobody is stressing."

Your girlfriends should be your accountability squad. If we can swap recipes, hair tips, and Tik Tok dances, we can swap strategies for stacking our paper.

With kids: Kids pick up on more than we think. If all they ever hear is, "We don't have it," or "Don't worry about it," they grow up scared or clueless about money. Change the narrative. Teach them what you wish you had known. Let them watch you budget or explain what bills are.

- At the grocery store... "We're buying the off-brand today because it's cheaper, and that means we save money for things we really want and need later."
- At home... "This is how much the light bill costs. Every time you leave a light on, that's money wasted."

- <u>With teenagers..</u> "Let's look at your first paycheck together. Here's what taxes took out. Here's what you should save before you spend."

Make money conversations normal, not taboo.

With yourself: This might sound silly, but sometimes you've got to check yourself out loud. Check-in every week. Ask...

- "What did I do this week for future me?"
- "Do I spend like the woman I want to be or the woman I'm trying to grow out of?"

With your partner: This one can be tricky, but it's necessary. Money issues are one of the top reasons relationships end, not because couples don't have it, but because they don't talk about it.

- Early dating: "Hey, I like to be smart with my money. How do you usually handle yours?"
- In a relationship: "What's your credit situation? I don't want any surprises if we build together."
- Married or long-term: "Let's set a money date tonight. We'll look at the bills, the goals, and maybe even dream a little about what we're building."

If your partner gets defensive, that's a red flag. If someone can share their body, their house, and their future with you but not their bank statement, you need to pause.

Talking about money doesn't make you greedy. It makes you grown. Silence is how generational curses get passed down.

Conversation is how generational wealth gets built.

Step 4: Know your numbers.

At any given moment, you should know:

- Your credit score
- Your checking balance
- Your savings balance
- How much you're putting toward retirement

Some would say this is being obsessed with money. I challenge you to reframe this method of thinking. Knowing your complete financial picture, having real conversations with your loved ones, and being financially responsible is not being obsessed with money. That's being in control.

The Friend Who "Didn't Do Money"

I had a friend who once told me, "Girl, I don't do money. It stresses me out." She would swipe her card and pray. She never opened her credit card statements because she, "Didn't want to see the damage." And for years, she got by until her car broke down. No savings. Maxed out cards. Credit too low for a loan.

That $800 repair bill turned into a financial nightmare. She had to borrow money, missed work, fell behind on bills, and her credit score dropped even lower because she couldn't make minimum credit card payments.

All because she didn't want to "do money."

I hate to be the bearer of bad news, you don't get to opt out of money. Whether you face it or not, money is happening. And when you don't face it, it controls you.

The Takeaway

Your purse is more than a fashion statement. It's a reflection of how you value yourself and your future. Every dollar in or out is a choice, and those choices add up to either financial freedom or frustration.

You deserve freedom. You deserve options. You deserve to know what's in your purse, and how to grow it.

So let's agree on this before we go any further...financial education is not optional. It's your birthright.

Say it with me: "I deserve to be financially free, and I'm ready to learn how."

Quick Exercise:
Your Financial Temperature Check

Answer these questions.

What are my checking and savings account balances right now?

_____

_____

_____

_____

_____

Do I know my credit score (within 20 points)?

_____

_____

_____

_____

_____

How much do I have saved for emergencies?

_____

_____

_____

_____

_____

When's the last time I checked my retirement account balance?

_____

_____

_____

_____

_____

*If you struggle with more than one of these, that's not fail-
ure...that's your starting line.*

Chapter 2
Rent Or Sunday Brunch?

Develop A Budget: Prioritize Saving
For Yourself, Even If You Start Small

I t's Friday afternoon, and your direct deposit just hit. You open your banking app, see your account balance, and breathe a sigh of relief. For a split second, it feels like freedom. You've been waiting all week for this money to land. Before you can even close the app, here comes the group chat.

"Ladies, brunch Sunday? I found a spot with bottomless mimosas."

"*Ooooh* yes, I'm in! I need a break."

"Y'all, I just booked a quick flight for next month. Tickets are cheap right now."

You type "Yes!" and your thumb is hovering over the send button. In the back of your mind, you remember your rent is due in four days. The light bill that you pushed off? Still waiting. The car payment? Coming next week.

But the temptation is real. Brunch is fun, and bills are boring. New clothes are exciting, and groceries are routine. A vacation will make you feel alive, while paying the water bill just keeps you alive.

Here's the truth...in that moment, most of us don't stop to ask, "What does future me need?" We're too busy asking, "What will make me feel good right now?"

Let me be clear, I'm not anti-fun. I believe in joy, laughter, and treating yourself. However, too often our "treat yourself" comes before we've taken care of "secure yourself." That's why so many women are walking around with the freshest set of nails, the prettiest wigs, the flyest outfits, and the most stressed out finances.

Sis, you don't have to choose between beauty and bills

forever. You do have to learn how to prioritize, because if you can't tell your money where to go, it will always run off and leave you broke.

Why Budgeting Matters

Budgeting has a bad reputation. We hear the word "budget," and immediately picture saying "no" to everything fun. No nails. No Starbucks. No vacations. Nothing but rice, beans, and bills.

That's not budgeting. That's punishment.

A budget isn't saying "no" to life. It's about learning to say "yes" on purpose. Think of it this way...if you don't budget, your money is like an untrained puppy. It runs wild, tears up your shoes, makes messes everywhere, and you spend all your energy cleaning up after it. However, when you train that puppy, by giving it boundaries, routines, and structure, it behaves. And it knows where it belongs. And suddenly, life gets calmer. That's what a budget does. It calms your money.

Another way to look at it is your budget is your financial mirror. It shows you the truth, whether you like it or not. If your money is slipping through your fingers, the mirror won't lie. And just like stepping on the scale before starting a new health plan, facing the truth can be uncomfortable but it's the only way you can change.

Here's why it matters:

- **Budgets protect your priorities.** Rent gets paid. Groceries stay stocked. Gas is in the car. The lights stay on. You never have to wonder, "Will I make it this month?"
- **Budgets give you guilt free fun.** When you've already saved and already paid the bills, that extra $50 for nails or that weekend trip is pure enjoyment, not diminished by underlying stress.
- **Budgets create freedom.** Freedom from overdraft fees. Freedom from borrowing money. Freedom from that pit in your stomach when you swipe your card and pray.

Let's talk about that for a second. The average overdraft fee in America is about $35. Most banks will hit you with that fee multiple times in one day if several transactions bounce. I've seen women lose $150 in one day to overdraft fees. That's money that could have gone to real needs like groceries or gas. Across the U.S., overdraft fees add up to billions every year. That's money we literally give away because we don't have a plan.

Most importantly, budgets help you pay yourself first. Here's the trap...if you wait until you have "leftover money" to save, there will never be leftovers. Life will always find a way to eat up every dollar.

I once worked with a woman who told me, "I'll start saving when I make more money." Years later, after her income had doubled, her savings account was still empty. Why? Because her lifestyle kept expanding right along with her paycheck. Without a budget, she spent everything she made, no matter how much it was.

Saving $20 before you do anything else is more powerful than spending $200 and then promising to "catch up next time."

Budgeting forces you to put your future first. Even if you have to start small. Especially if you start small.

Let me put it to you this way, a budget is like a GPS for your money. You wouldn't just hop in the car for a road trip and "see where you end up." You'd put the destination's address in your GPS first. Your budget is that destination's address. Without it, you'll always end up lost.

So ask yourself, where do you want your money to take you? If the answer is "somewhere better than I am now," then you need a budget. Not to trap you. Not to punish you. But to guide you.

Janean's Story: Starting Small

In 2004, I found myself as a single mother, starting fresh in Atlanta, Georgia, with my 4-year-old daughter by my side. I had just left a long-term relationship with her father, and it felt like stepping into the unknown. I didn't have any family or friends nearby, just the two of us facing a new city together. It was a terrifying and challenging time; I was solely responsible for everything such as rent, car payments, childcare, and insurance, leaving little room for savings.

Shortly after arriving in Atlanta, I began training at a local bank. During one of the classes, we discussed savings accounts and how to get started. The bank offered an automated savings program that allowed me to contribute as little as $20 directly from my paycheck. I thought, "Why not? If I don't see the money, it won't hurt me." So, I set it up, having it automatically deposited into a savings account, and honestly, I forgot about it.

Before I knew it, I had over $500 saved by the end of the year. It may not seem like a lot to some, but that money became my emergency fund. With it, I was able to invest in a Certificate of Deposit that offered a higher interest rate, allowing my savings to grow over time. A few years later, I used that money to open a college savings plan for my daughter.

Looking back, I realize that sometimes you have to make sacrifices and take small steps to achieve your long-term goals. It's all about playing the long game, even when the journey feels daunting.

Practical Steps: How to Budget Like a Boss

Here is how you start taking control:

Step 1: Track Every Dollar

- For one month, write down (or use an app) to see exactly where your money goes. Coffee, gas, hair, lunch, all of it!
- You might be shocked. The "I don't have any money" story often turns into "I have money, I just spend it in the wrong places."

Step 2: Prioritize Needs First

- Rent/mortgage, utilities, groceries, transportation, minimum debt payments.
- These are non-negotiables. They keep your life running.

Step 3: Pay Yourself Second

- Before the nails, before brunch, before Amazon... save something. Even if it's $20 a paycheck. Make it automatically go from your main checking account to a savings account so you don't even think about it.
- This isn't leftover money. This is first choice money. This is you putting yourself and your future first.

Step 4: Give Yourself Play Money (Guilt-free)

- Budget for the fun stuff. If you want nails, trips, or Target runs, put a number on it. When the play money is gone, it's gone. That way you enjoy a little shopping splurge without any guilt.
- Be careful here not to overindulge. Like I said, when the play money is gone, it's gone!

Step 5: Review And Adjust

- A budget is not set in stone; it's not a prison. It's a living, breathing reflection of your life. Review it monthly and tweak as needed.
- This shouldn't take more than 20 or 30 minutes a month so don't avoid it or treat it like a homework project. Put your big girl panties on and get it done.

Subscription Overload

One of my clients swore up and down she didn't have any money to save. She sat across from me, arms folded, and said, "Janean, I'm living paycheck to paycheck. There is nothing left."

So, I asked her to pull up her bank statement. We scrolled together, and sis, let me tell you...it read like the credits at the end of a Marvel movie! Subscription after subscription after subscription.

Netflix. Hulu. Disney+. Apple TV. BET+. Amazon Prime. Spotify. A makeup box. A hair product box. Even a "mystery snack" box from overseas. And the kicker? She hadn't logged into half of them in months. She couldn't even remember the password to Disney+. When I added it all up, she was spending $259 a month on stuff she wasn't even using. That's not pocket change, that's a car payment. That's somebody's grocery budget. That's gas money for a whole month!

Here is where the math gets real.

- $259 a month x 12 months = $3,108 a year, gone.
- Over 5 years? That's $15,540. Do you know what $15,540 could be? A down payment on a house. A fully paid-off used car. Tuition for your child's first year of college.
- And if she had invested just $259 a month into an index fund instead of snacks and streaming? In 10 years, at a modest 7% return, she'd have over $45,000!

She sat there wide eyed and said, "I had no idea I was spending that much." That's when I told her, "You don't have a money problem. You have a money leak."

We cancelled everything but the three she actually used. That freed up $145 a month...money she thought she didn't have. She set it to auto transfer into her savings account, and six months later she had $870 saved. A year later, she had $1,740.

And here's the best part! She told me, "I don't even miss them. I don't miss what I wasn't using, but I love seeing that savings account grow!" That's the power of a budget. It exposes the leaks in your purse. Sometimes the reason you "can't save" isn't because you don't earn enough, it's because your money is quietly tiptoeing out the back door in $19.99 chunks.

The Takeaway

Sis, budgeting isn't about restriction, it's about elevation. When you budget, you give yourself the power to handle your responsibilities, save for your future, and still enjoy your life without shame.

So the next time you are choosing between your rent and getting your nails done, remember your nails will grow back but the eviction will set you back.

Say it with me: "I choose to pay myself first, even if I start small."

And let me add this, every dollar you budget is a declaration. It's you telling your money, "I run this." It's you breaking free from the cycle of living check to check. It's you deciding that future you deserves better than leftovers.

No matter where you are financially, you are not too late. You are not too far gone. You are not "bad with money." You are a woman taking control, one paycheck at a time. Every step, no matter how small, is proof that you're building the life you deserve.

Affirm this with me: "I am disciplined. I am deserving. I am wealthy. Wisdom and my purse will reflect my priorities."

Quick Exercise:
Purse Priorities

Answer the questions below.

Write down every expense you pay in a month.

_____

_____

_____

_____

_____

_____

_____

_____

_____

_____

_____

Sort them. Which ones keep you secure and stable (needs)? Which ones make life fun (wants)?

NEEDS

_____

_____

_____

_____

_____

_____

_____

_____

_____

_____

_____

_____

_____

_____

_____

WANTS

_____

_____

_____

_____

_____

_____

_____

_____

_____

_____

_____

_____

_____

_____

_____

Now ask yourself if your paycheck was cut in half tomorrow, what would stay? What would go?

_____

_____

_____

_____

_____

This simple exercise will show you if your purse is out of order and exactly where you need to tighten up.

Chapter 3
Sis, Stress Isn't Cute

The Impact of Financial Wellness
On Mental Health

I magine this. You're standing in line at the grocery store. Your cart isn't overflowing, just a few basics. Some bread, fruit, milk, and chicken. The cashier rings it up, and the total flashes: $52.43.

You slide your debit card and hold your breath. The machine beeps. Declined. You try another card. Same result. The line behind you was growing, and you can feel the heat rising in your face. You force a laugh, mumble something about "bank errors" and ask the cashier to put some things back. Inside, you feel like disappearing.

That kind of embarrassment sticks to you. It follows you home when you replay it over and over. You don't tell anybody, because who wants to admit they couldn't afford groceries? Instead, you smile in social media selfies while hiding the fact that you're eating ramen for dinner...again.

Or maybe it's this: your friend group is planning a trip. The group chat is popping with hotel links, excursions, and outfit ideas. Everyone's excited, dropping memes and planning itineraries. You know you can't afford it. Instead of admitting that, you make excuses. "Work's too busy," or "I'm not really into that location." Deep down, you're embarrassed. You don't want them to know the truth which is that your bank account said no before you even had a chance to.

And sis, sometimes the embarrassment shows up even in small ways. Like when you avoid answering the phone because you're scared it's a bill collector. Or when you skip opening your mail because you know what's inside is another notice you don't want to face. Or when you turn down dates, outings, or opportunities not because you don't want to go but because you know your purse can't keep up.

That's the reality. Financial stress doesn't just live in your bank account, it shows up in your body, your confidence, and your relationships.

The Lesson: Money & Mental Health Are Connected

Money is more than just math. It's emotional. It's spiritual. It's mental. And when your money is a mess, your mind will be, too. Financial stress is sneaky because it creeps into areas that don't seem connected to money at first glance.

- **It eats at your confidence.** You start second-guessing yourself at work, in relationships, even in small decisions like whether you deserve a coffee or whether you can apply for that promotion. You're not alone. A 2025 Bankrate survey found that 43% of U.S. adults say money negatively affects their mental health, with anxiety, stress, and loss of sleep at the top of the list. And women? We are hit harder! Forty-five percent of women said money stress hurts their mental health compared to 41% of men.

- **It creates shame.** You avoid conversations, make excuses, and overcompensate by looking polished on the outside while you're falling apart inside. Some of us smile through brunch while silently praying our card won't decline. Shame convinces you that you're the only one struggling, even though millions are.

- **It fosters unhealthy relationships.** People stay in toxic partnerships because they "can't afford" to leave. Others cling to friendships where the currency is keeping up with appearances instead of true connection. That's not just my opinion. A 2022 National Health interview survey found that financial worries are strongly tied to psychological distress like anxiety and depression, especially for renters, low-income households, and single women.

- **It drains your energy.** Constant worry about money keeps you up at night, and exhaustion follows you everywhere. The bills might not be due yet, but the anxiety is always on time. The TIAA Institute even found that workers under high financial stress are more distracted, miss more days, and show up late more often than peers with stable finances.

Also the body keeps the score. Stress hormones don't know the difference between a bill collector calling and a lion chasing you...your body stays in fight-or-flight mode either way. Over time, that shows up as migraines, high blood pressure, digestive issues, weight gain, and insomnia.

What makes it worse? The cycle of worry. A 2024 Bankrate study found that people who said money hurt their mental health were three times more likely to have a bill late in the past month. That means the stress itself can lead to late payments, which creates more fees, which create more stress. It's a vicious loop.

Money stress isn't just inconvenient. It's dangerous and it chips away at your peace, your self-worth, and your health. It can make you feel like you're failing at life when really, you're just carrying more than anyone should have to without the right tools. And the biggest lie shame tells you is that you're the only one. You're not. The numbers prove it.

Janean's Story: Embarrassment in the Bank

A college friend of mine always had big dreams for her future. She married a great guy who was financially stable, and she felt secure in that. Unfortunately, she didn't have much discipline when it came to money. She thought that because her husband was good with finances, she could be carefree about it. That wasn't the case.

She loved dressing up in designer clothes—Chanel, Gucci, you name it. She always looked impeccable, but behind that polished exterior, there was a reality she was ignoring: she had no savings and no plan for retirement. I tried talking to her about it, but it was like my words just floated away.

Then one day, I received a frantic call from her. Everything had come crashing down. She was in deep trouble because she had been using credit cards to maintain her glamorous image, and the debt had spiraled out of control. The stress was taking a toll on her. She was losing weight, her hair was thinning, and sleepless nights had become the norm.

I gently reminded her that credit cards aren't a way to access extra money; they're just a tool that can lead to serious issues if mismanaged. I knew how much this was affecting her, especially in her marriage. The fear of admitting she needed help had led her to consider bankruptcy, all because of the shame of not seeking guidance sooner.

Sometimes, silence can be a silent killer. I urged her to break that silence and speak up. It's never easy to confront these challenges, but taking control of her financial life was the first step toward healing. We all need support. Asking for help can be the bravest decision we make.

Practical Steps: Protecting Your Mind & Money

So how do you build financial wellness that supports your mental health? Here's how.

Step 1: Name the Stress Out Loud

- Write down what's keeping you up at night about money. Is it debt? Bills? Not earning enough?
- Naming it takes away its power. What you won't face will always control you.
- *Example:* I worked with a woman who said she couldn't sleep because of her student loans. Once she wrote down the actual number and the interest rate, she realized it wasn't as impossible as she imagined. Seeing it clearly gave her a hint of relief.

Step 2: Create a "Peace Budget"

- This isn't just numbers. Build a budget that covers your basics, pays you first, and includes a small "joy fund." Knowing that you can afford a treat guilt-free reduces shame.

- *Example:* One client budgeted $20 a week for coffee and books. She told me, "It's not a lot, but it's the only thing I do just for me. Having that money set aside keeps me sane." And she was right, $20 is not a lot. However, for the peace of mind it gave her and the feeling of having a splurge, that $20 was more than worth it.

Step 3: Set Boundaries and Relationships

- *With friends...* If the outing isn't in your budget, say, "Not this time, but let's plan something affordable soon." Real friends respect it.

- *With partners...* Be honest about money stress. Don't let silence turn into resentment.

- *With yourself...* Stop the comparison game. Instagram is not a financial advisor. The people posting luxury trips often don't post the credit card bills behind them. You don't know what they have behind closed doors, you only see what they want you to see. It's all smoke and mirrors. You know *your* full story, let's be real with ourselves.

Step 4: Seek Support, Not Silence

- Therapy and financial coaching are both valid. Talking to a professional about money stress isn't weakness, it's wisdom.

- *Example:* A former coworker finally opened up to me about her sister being $10,000 in credit card debt. Instead of judging the confession, her sister said, "Girl, me, too." That conversation led them to work on paying down debt together, and both said the shame lifted instantly. This is also a way of having an accountability partner as you both work toward financial goals be it a savings account, increasing your credit score, paying down debt. Having someone to do it with keeps you motivated and on track.

Step 5: Celebrate Small Wins

- Paid off a credit card? Celebrate. Saved $100? Celebrate. Said "no" to a trip you couldn't afford? Celebrate. Every small victory builds confidence.
- *Example:* I once told a client to clap for herself every time she made a payment toward debt. She laughed, but after a while she said, "That silly clap made me feel proud instead of punished." You can do the same. Cheer yourself on and say to yourself out loud, "Girl, I am so proud of you! You did it!"

Staying for Security

I once counseled a woman who stayed in a toxic

relationship for years. Why? Because he paid the rent. She told me, "I don't love him, but I can't afford to leave."

Sis, that's financial bondage. And it's more common than people admit.

Every time he raised his voice, every time he disrespected her, every time he reminded her that he was the one keeping a roof over her head, she felt smaller and smaller. She had a good job, but between student loans, car payments, and helping her family, she was always broke by the end of the month. The thought of paying rent alone terrified her. So she stayed. Not out of love, but because of money.

She confessed to me that when friends asked why she was still with him, she'd shrug and say, "He's not that bad." Inside, she felt trapped. That's what money stress does, it convinces you to accept less than you deserve because the alternative feels impossible. Thankfully, something shifted for her. We sat down and created a simple budget. She started small, cutting out things she didn't miss. A couple of subscriptions, take-out three nights a week, a new outfit every payday. That freed up $500 a month. She opened a savings account and named it her "freedom fund" and promised herself she wouldn't touch it unless it was to leave.

Seeing that first $500 saved lit a fire in her. She realized she really could do this! By the time she had $1,500, she was standing taller. She started saying "no" to his disrespect because she knew she had options. And the day she finally packed her bags and left, she didn't just walk out of her relationship, she walked out of shame into freedom. That's the power of financial wellness. It's not just about numbers on the spreadsheet. It's about giving yourself choices. Choices to leave, to stay, to rest, to build...without fear, without begging, without settling.

Takeaway

Financial wellness isn't just about paying bills. It's about protecting your peace, your confidence, your future. Money stress is heavy, but you don't have to carry it forever.

Say it with me: "My money does not define me. I define my money."

Affirm this truth: "I deserve financial freedom and emotional peace. I am not my overdraft. I am not my debt. I am not my shame. I am worthy of wealth, worthy of rest, and worthy of relationships that honor me."

Quick Exercise:
Your Money + Mind Check-in

Answer these questions.

What money situation embarrasses me the most right now?

_____

_____

_____

_____

_____

_____

What lie have I believed about myself because of money? ("I'm bad with money," "I'll never get out of debt,")

_____

_____

_____

_____

_____

What's one small win I can create this month to prove that lie wrong?

_____

_____

_____

_____

_____

<u>*Example*</u>

- *Embarrassment:* My card declined at dinner last week.
- *Lie:* "I'm always broke, no matter what I do."
- *Small win:* Track my spending this week and move $20 into savings first to prove I can make smart money choices.

This exercise will help you see the connection between your wallet and your well-being.

Chapter 4
Sis, What's The Plan

Establishing A Clear Financial Vision

Picture this. You wake up on Monday morning, groaning at the alarm, rushing to get to work. You get paid on Friday, the bills are due by Tuesday, and the weekend plans are already being plotted in your group chat. You're on autopilot, chasing the next check just to survive the next cycle.

You don't really know where your money is going. You just know it disappears. Direct deposits land, and like clockwork, the auto-drafts hit. Car note. Rent. Student loans. Utilities. And that's if you're bold enough to have auto-draft. Otherwise, you manually pay out bills and watch your account dwindle. A few impulse swipes here, a dinner there. By the time you look up, you're wondering, *Where did it all go?*

If someone stopped you right now and asked, "Sis, what's your financial vision?" what would you say? Would you have a clear answer? Or would you stumble over your words, "*Ummm...uhhh...*I just want to be comfortable?"

Too many of us are living without a plan. And here's the kicker, when you don't have a plan, life will make one for you. I'm pretty sure life's plan is not one you'd be excited to text home about. The landlord's plan, the bank's plan, Sallie Mae's plan, the credit card company's plan. Spoiler alert...none of their plans are designed to make you wealthy or contribute to your final freedom at all.

One lady I asked this question answered me by saying, "I'm just trying to get by." She was in her 40s, working two jobs, always tired. She said, "As long as the lights stay on and the rent gets paid, I'm ok."

"What about retirement?" I followed up. "What about owning your home? What about leaving something for your kids?"

Her response was silence. Nobody had ever asked her those questions. From the way she looked down in defeat, it seemed she hadn't even asked herself.

Another client was the opposite. She had all the outward signs of success...designer clothes, luxury car, vacation. Yet when we sat down, she admitted she didn't have a single savings account. No investments. No emergency fund. Her answer about having a financial plan was similar to the first lady's, "I'm just living life as it comes."

Sis, let me tell you something, if you don't define your destination, you will always drift. Drifting doesn't lead to financial freedom. Drifting leads to exhaustion. To working until you can't work anymore. To waking up at 65 and realizing you've spent decades moving but never arriving.

It's like getting in the car with no address in the GPS. You're driving, the engine's running, the wheels are turning, but you're lost. You might hit a nice road or two, but you'll never get to the place you deserve.

Now, contrast that with someone who has vision. A woman who says, "In five years, I want to be debt-free. In ten years, I want to own a home. By retirement, I want to travel twice a year without worrying about money." That vision isn't just words, it becomes a map. Once you have the map, your money decisions start making sense. You can stop asking, "Can, I afford brunch?" and start asking, "Does brunch fit into my bigger vision?"

Let me put it to you straight. Having a financial vision is not optional. Vision is survival. Vision is wealth.

Why Financial Vision Matters

Money without vision is like water with no container. It just spills everywhere. A clear financial vision gives your money purpose.

Here's why it matters.

1. **Vision gives you focus.** When you know what you want, it's easier to say "no" to distractions. You stop swiping your card just because something is cute in the moment. You start asking, "Does this get me closer to or further from my goal?"

2. **Vision builds confidence.** Have you ever noticed how people with confidence walk differently? They stand taller and speak clearer. The same is true with money. When you can articulate where you're going financially, you feel grounded. Instead of hiding from conversations about investments or retirement, you can step into them with confidence.

3. **Vision keeps you motivated when life gets tough.** Bills are boring. Sacrifices are hard. When you have a vision like owning your own home, sending your kids to college debt-free, or retiring early, those sacrifices feel worth it. You're not just saying "no" to shoes; you're saying "yes" to freedom.

4. **Vision prevents unhealthy cycles.** Without vision, you'll repeat the same poor money management behaviors over and over, just with different outfits. Same debt, same stress, same paycheck-to-paycheck struggle. Vision forces you to break the loop because you're moving

toward something bigger.

Let's be real, women especially need vision. Why?

- Because we live longer.
- Because we still earn less.
- Because we carry more of the family burden.

That means if we don't plan, we're setting ourselves up to struggle during the (future) times when we should be resting.

The numbers don't lie. A Fidelity Investments survey found that 67% of women want to learn more about investing, but only 29% actually feel confident doing it. Why? Because nobody helped us connect the dots between today's dollars and tomorrow's dreams.

Vision isn't about being rich tomorrow, get that out of your head. That is not what I'm saying. Vision is about building step-by-step. It's not about having $100,000 in the bank today. It's about knowing that every dollar you save, every debt you pay, every investment you make is a brick in the house you're building.

When you lack vision, embarrassment fills the gap. You make choices based on how they'll look to other people instead of how they'll serve your future. You buy the purse to prove you're doing well. You go on the trip so you don't look "broke." However, with vision, you realize that saying no today is not punishment, it's preparation.

Here's the challenge, stop asking, "What do I want right now?" and start asking, "What do I want my money to do for me five years from now? Ten years from now? Twenty?"

Vision doesn't mean you won't enjoy today. It just means you'll enjoy tomorrow even more.

Janean's Story: Seeing The Bigger Picture

When I moved to Atlanta with my four-year-old daughter, I had a clear vision in mind. I knew our time in that apartment would be short, just a year, but I wanted so much more for her. I dreamed of a place where she could grow up surrounded by friends in a community where she could build lasting relationships.

Every penny counted. I made sacrifices—celebrating bonuses at work by putting them toward our future instead of splurging on things we didn't really need. I focused on the essentials, always keeping our goal in sight. The thought of homeownership felt daunting; I had no idea where to start. But I rolled up my sleeves, did my research, and learned as much as I could.

It wasn't easy, and it took longer than I had initially hoped. By the time my daughter turned seven, we had finally moved into our very own home. It was a moment of triumph for us—a place filled with love and safety, where she could thrive. As a single parent, it felt like a true victory. I couldn't have been prouder of the journey we had taken together.

Practical Steps: Creating Your
Financial Vision

Step 1: Define Your "Why"

Every vision starts with a why. If your why isn't strong enough, your vision won't hold when life gets tough. For example, one of my clients said her why was "to save money." That wasn't enough. When she dug deeper, she said, "I want to save money because I don't ever want my kids to see the lights cut off like I did growing up." That was powerful. That why kept her going even when her friends were out shopping.

Your why should give you chills. It should bring tears to your eyes. Because when brunch invites hit or when Instagram tries to convince you to buy things you don't need, your why will be louder than the temptation.

Step 2: Set SMART Goals

General goals don't work. "I want to be rich" sounds nice, but there is no action behind it. SMART goals are Specific, Measurable, Achievable, Relevant, Time-bound...and they keep you accountable.

Instead of saying, "I want to save money," try "I will save $5,000 in two years by setting aside $210 every month." That's concrete. That's trackable.

Say your goal is to get out of debt to the tune of $12,000. Just saying, "I want to get out of debt isn't going to cut it. By making it SMART, you can say, "By paying $300 a month, I'll be debt-free in 40 months. Suddenly, what may have previously felt impossible is now possible, and you have a 3-year plan.

Step 3: Break It Down

Big goals can be overwhelming. That's why so many people quit before they start. Breaking them into smaller pieces makes them manageable. Think of it like eating a cake. You don't swallow it whole, you eat it slice by slice. Saving $20,000 for a down payment sounds very scary! However, saving $100 a week sounds doable.

One of my clients wanted an emergency fund of $1,000. Instead of waiting for a big windfall, she set aside $25 a week. And less than a year, she had it. She told me, "I never missed the $25, but I love the feeling of having that position."

Step 4: Visualize It

Your brain responds to images. That's why vision boards work. When you see it daily, it trains your subconscious to believe it's possible. One of my clients printed out a picture of the house she wanted and taped it to her bathroom mirror. Every morning, she brushed her teeth looking at that house. It kept her focused. Two years later, she sent me a photo of herself standing in front of that exact model home.

Visualization doesn't just inspire, it rewires your brain. Studies show people who write down and visualize goals are 42% more likely to achieve them.

Step 5: Check-in Regularly

Visions fail when they're written once and forgotten. You have to revisit them, tweak them, and celebrate progress along the way.

Think of it as a GPS. If you make the wrong turn, the GPS doesn't yell at you "you failed." It simply says, "recalculating." That's how your financial vision should look. Missed a month? Unexpected expense? That's not failure, that's recalculation.

One woman I coached wrote her financial goals on sticky notes and put them on her fridge. Every time she paid off a debt or saved a milestone, she'd move that sticky note to the "done" side. Watching them pile up gave her more momentum than any app ever could.

Takeaway

Sis, drifting is not destiny. You were not put on this earth just to work, pay bills, and die. You were created to thrive, to build, to enjoy, to rest. Without a vision, you will always settle for survival when God intended you for abundance.

Money without vision is wasted potential, and you know I'm not lying. It leaks away on shoes, trips, and take out...none of which will be here 10 years from now. Money with a vision? That's legacy. That's home ownership. That's retirement without fear. That's scholarships for your children and vacations where you can actually relax instead of stressing about the credit card bill waiting at home.

Your financial vision is not just about you. It's about your children, your family, your community. When you save, invest, and build, you are planting trees that will give shade to generations you'll never meet.

So let me remind you that a lack of vision is not a lack of worth. You are not "bad with money" you are not "too far behind." You are simply a woman who has never been given the tools until now. This is your turning point.

Say it with me:

- "I am not lost. I have direction."
- "I am not broke. I am building."
- "I am not behind. I am becoming."

Affirm this truth, "My vision is clear. My money obeys my vision. My future will reflect the choices I make today."

Every dollar you touch is a soldier. Put your soldiers to work. March them toward your goals. Train them to fight for your freedom. The life you desire is already waiting on you. All that's left is for you to claim it.

Quick Exercise:
Your Money Vision Statement

Write a 2-3 sentence vision statement starting with:

In the next 12 months, I will...

_____

_____

_____

_____

_____

_____

In 3 years, I will...

_____

_____

_____

_____

_____

_____

In 5 years, I will...

_____

_____

_____

_____

_____

_____

In 10 years, I will...

_____

_____

_____

_____

_____

_____

Post it on your mirror, fridge, or in your journal.

Chapter 5
Sis, Will You Still Be Working at 70?

The Necessity of a Retirement Plan

Picture this... You walk into your favorite coffee shop at 7:00 a.m. The line is long, the baristas are hustling, and behind the counter you spot a woman in her late 60s. Her hands shake slightly as she hands out change. She's smiling, but her eyes looked tired. She's not there for "something to do" in retirement. She's there because she has to be.

Having a conversation with a beautiful woman in this situation, she told me, "I thought Social Security would cover me. It doesn't even cover my rent." She was 68, working 30 hours a week on her feet. Not because she wanted extra money for vacations or grandkids gifts'. She did it because she had no choice.

Now, picture another woman, also in her late 60s. She's waking up at that same 7:00 a.m., only she's at home, sipping coffee on her porch, planning a trip with her girlfriends, deciding which grandchild to spoil next. The difference between these two women isn't luck. It isn't "marrying rich." It's planning.

Let me be real, too many of us are headed for the first woman's reality. We avoid thinking about retirement because it feels far away. We tell ourselves, "I'll deal with that later." However, later comes faster than you think. And later doesn't care if you're ready or not.

I also think of a woman I counseled who worked faithfully for 40 years. She raised her kids, supported her husband, kept food on the table, and always said, "I'll worry about me later." Guess what? Later came...only she hadn't saved a dime. Her only option was to move in with her adult daughter. On the outside, she told people, "It's nice to be close to family." Behind closed doors, she admitted the truth which was she felt like a burden. Every grocery trip, her daughter covered. Every utility bill, she chipped in for. Every small request she made to her daughter for gas money chipped away at her pride. She said, "I spent my whole life taking care of others, and now I can't even take care of myself."

Hearing that broke me. It wasn't that she had not worked hard all her life. She had worked harder than most. It was about a lack of planning, a lack of someone telling her, "Sis, you need a retirement plan. Not later. *Now*."

What does it look like when we don't plan?

- Working until our bodies give out.
- Living on Social Security, which averages around $1,900 a month...barely enough to cover rent in most cities.
- Depending on adult children, which creates stress and guilt for everyone.
- Sacrificing dignity because the money simply isn't there.

As painful as it is to accept, retirement planning gaps hit women, especially Black women, the hardest. Why? Because we live longer, earn less, and often pause our careers to care for family. That means we need more money for retirement, yet end up with less.

It's like running a marathon where the men start at mile five and we start at mile zero with ankle weights. We're still expected to finish strong. That's why this conversation is urgent.

Simply put, if you don't have a retirement plan, you are gambling your future on hope. And hope is not a financial strategy.

Why Retirement Planning Is Non-negotiable

Retirement is not optional. The day will come when you can't, don't want to, or simply shouldn't have to work anymore. If you don't plan, that day will feel like a crisis instead of a celebration.

Here's why it matters:

1. **We live longer.** Women live in an average of five years longer than men. That means our retire-ment savings have to stretch further. If you retire at 65 and live to 85, that's 20 years of bills. Let's be honest, 20 years of bills without a steady paycheck feels like a nightmare if you're unprepared. It's not just about "making it" to retirement, it's about surviving in retirement. Longevity is a blessing; however, without your financial needs met, it can feel like punishment.

2. **We earn less and save less.** The gender pay gap is real, and it hits Black women the hardest. We earn about $0.64 for every dollar a white man makes. Over a lifetime, that adds up to hundreds of thousands of dollars in lost wages. And lost wages mean lost savings, lost investments, lost opportunities. That's not laziness, that's systemic inequity. Even with the gap, planning helps us close the distance. Without a plan, the gap becomes a canyon.

3. **Social Security isn't enough.** I need you to hear me loud and clear, Social Security was never meant to be your full retirement plan. It was designed as a supplement. In 2025, the average Social Security check is about $1,900 a month. That sounds ok until you start subtracting. Rent

in many cities? $1,500 or more. Groceries for just one person? Easily $400 to $500 a month. Utilities, gas, subscriptions? You're already in the red. That's before we even talk about enjoying life. Without a retirement plan, Social Security is not security at all. It's survival on scraps.

4. **Inflation is real.** Groceries, gas, rent, healthcare... all of it costs more each year. A gallon of milk in 2000 was $2.79. Today, it's closer to $4.50. What you think you need today will not be enough tomorrow. The same $1,900 Social Security check will buy less and less each year. Without a plan, you'll always feel like you're drowning in rising prices.

5. **Health care will be your biggest expense.** As we age, health care costs rise. A Fidelity study estimated that the average 65-year-old couple retiring today will need about $315,000 just for healthcare expenses in retirement. Think about that number. That's not vacations. That's not spoiling grandbabies. That's doctors, prescriptions, surgeries, and treatments. And for women who live longer, those costs are even higher. Without planning, health care alone can wipe you out.

6. **Retirement planning protects your dignity.** Money stress in your 20s and 30s is embarrassing. Money stress in your 70s is devastating. No one wants to feel like a burden. No one wants to rely on their kids for every little thing. Nobody wants to move into a spare bedroom when they dreamed of traveling or resting. Planning isn't just about numbers, it's about dignity. It's about freedom. It's about being able to choose how you live out the last decades of your life.

Now let's look at some real numbers:

- About 25% of Americans have no retirement savings at all.
- Among those who do, the median 401(k) balance for people in their 50s is only about $57,000. That's not enough to last even two years for most households.
- When we look specifically at Black women, the retirement gap is even wider. According to a 2022 TIA study, Black women are less likely to have access to employer sponsored retirement plans, and when they do, they save at lower rates, not because they want to, but because competing financial pressure (caregiving, wage gaps) eat up their income.

This is why I say retirement planning isn't a luxury, it's a necessity. It's not something you do "if" you can. It's something you must do to protect yourself.

Why Women, Especially, Need A Vision

Culturally, many of us grew up watching our mommas, aunties, and grandmas sacrifice for everyone else. They worked, they cooked, they raised kids, they tithed, they gave. Very few were taught to pay themselves first. The result? Too many Black women are hitting retirement age exhausted and broke.

And the saddest part? These are the same women who carried entire families on their backs. Who bailed out cousins, raised grandkids, kept churches running, and fed neighborhoods. They deserved ease, but without a plan, they just got struggle.

I don't want that for you. I don't want your story to end with you working until your body gives out or depending on someone else for survival. I want your story to be one of rest, joy, and abundance, because you dared to plan.

Here is the hopeful part, it's never too late to start! Whether you're 25 or 55, you can take steps today that your future self will thank you for. The key is to start. Compound interest doesn't care if you're shy, scared, or skeptical. It works quietly in the background, multiplying your dollars as long as you give it time.

Let me break it down:

- Invest $200 a month starting at 25 and by 65, you'll have over $500,000 (assuming a 7% return)
- Start at 40 $\rightarrow$ $240,000
- Start at 50 $\rightarrow$ still about $115,000

Is it easier the earlier you start? Yes. I want to impress upon you that starting late is still better than not starting at all.

Janean's Story: Watching The Difference

When I was a young banker, I saw two women retire in the same year. One had a plan, the other didn't.

The first woman came in with her portfolio neatly organized. She had a 401(k), a small pension, and savings she'd built over 30 years. She was smiling, excited, talking about cruises and volunteer work.

The second woman came in with tears in her eyes. She had no savings. Her Social Security barely covered her rent. She said, "I guess I'll just keep working until I can't anymore."

That broke me. Two women, same age, same city, completely different realities. The only difference was vision and planning.

That's when I made my vow... I will never let another woman sit across from me and say, "Nobody told me."

Practical Steps: Building Your Retirement Plan

Retirement planning sounds intimidating because nobody ever sat us down and broke it down in plain language. Banks talk over our heads, employers hand us thick packets full of jargon, and most of us just check a box on our benefits form and hope for the best. Hope is not a strategy. Here is how to take control, step by step, no finance degree required.

Step 1: Know Your Number

You can't hit a target you haven't named. Most people say, "I just want enough to be comfortable." We've established "comfortable" is not a number. A clear financial vision starts with knowing how much you'll actually need.

A simple rule to use to calculate your number is called the "25x Rule." Take your annual expense total and multiply it by 25. That's roughly what you'll need to retire comfortably.

- *Example:* If you spend $40,000 a year, you'll need about $1 million.
- If you spend $60,000 annually, you'll need about $1.5 million.

Does that sound big? Probably. Don't panic...you don't have to save it all today. The point is to give you a realistic destination. What you measure, you can also manage.

Step 2: Start Where You Are

Too many women don't start because they feel behind. "I'll never save a million, so why bother?" That's shame talking, not strategy.

Start small. If you can only do $50 a month, do that. If you can only do $200, do that. Don't let comparison paralyze you. Progress is progress.

I had a client who started with $25 per paycheck. She called it her "retirement jar." At first, it felt silly like, what would such a small amount do? After a year, she had $650. Then, she got a raise, bumped it up to $100 a month, and in three years she had over $4,000. What seemed like "too little to matter" became her first big win.

Step 3: Use Retirement Accounts

This is where your money really works for you.

Retirement accounts come with tax advantages that make your dollar stretch further. Here's the breakdown in plain English:

- **401(k):** Offered through many employers. You put in money before taxes, and it grows tax deferred until retirement. If your employer offers a match, take it. That's free money.
  - *Example*: If you earn $60,000 and contribute 5% ($3,000 a year), and your employer matches 5%, you've just doubled your money without lifting a finger.
- **IRA (Individual Retirement Account):** Great option if your job doesn't offer a 401(k). You can contribute up to a set amount each year (in 2025, it's $7,000 for most people).
- **Roth IRA:** You pay taxes on the money now, but when you retire, your withdrawals are tax free. That means every dollar you see in retirement is yours to keep.

Pick one and start. Don't let the alphabet soup confuse you. The main thing is to get in the game.

Step 4: Automate It

The easiest way to save is not to think about it. Automate your contributions so the money goes straight from your paycheck or bank account into your retirement fund. When saving is automatic, it becomes a bill you pay yourself...non-negotiable, just like our rent or utilities.

One of my clients who swore she "couldn't save" found out she absolutely could. Once we automated $150 out of her paycheck, she didn't even notice it was gone. Six months later, she had $900 saved and asked, "Why didn't I do that sooner?"

Step 5: Don't Fall For The Myths

There are a few lies that keep women from building wealth for retirement. Let's bust them.

- *"I'll just work forever."* Sis, even if you want to, your body might not agree. Health, layoffs, or caregiving responsibilities often cut careers short.
- *"My kids will take care of me."* That's not fair to them, and honestly, most adult children are struggling with their own bills. Love them enough to not add that burden.
- *"Social Security will be enough."* As we already saw earlier in this chapter, it won't. Treat Social Security as a side dish, not the main meal.

Step 6: Harness Compound Interest

Compound interest is your best friend. It's money making money while you sleep. The earlier you start, the more powerful it is. Time is the magic ingredient. Even if you're starting late, consistency plus compound interest will surprise you.

Step 7: Check-in and Adjust

Your retirement plan isn't one and done. Life changes. Salaries grow. Expenses shift. Review your progress at least once a year. Increase contributions when you get a raise. Adjust if your goals change.

Remember the GPS and how it recalculates after a wrong turn? Yeah, this is where that comes into play. Your plan should do the same. Flexibility keeps you moving, even when life doesn't go as planned.

Step 8: Celebrate Milestones

Retirement planning is long-term, but don't wait 30 years to clap for yourself. Celebrate every win. Paid off a credit card so you can put more toward your 401(k)? Celebrate. Reached $10,000 in savings? Celebrate. Those small victories keep you motivated for the bigger picture.

Your retirement plan is not about being perfect, it's about being intentional. Every step you take is a declaration that your future matters.

Takeaway

Retirement isn't a dream; it's a destination. Every dollar you save is a mile closer. Don't let fear or shame keep you from planning. Don't wait for "someday." Someday is today.

Say it with me: "I deserve rest. I deserve freedom. I deserve a retirement filled with joy, not stress."

Affirm this truth: "I am building my future with wisdom. My money will provide for me when my body no longer can. I will retire with dignity, peace, and abundance."

Quick Exercise:
Your Retirement Snapshot

Answer these questions.

How much do I spend a year right now?

_____

_____

_____

_____

_____

Multiply that by 25. That's your retirement target.

_____

_____

_____

_____

_____

_____

How much am I currently saving each month?

_____

_____

_____

_____

_____

What's one step I can take to increase it this year?

_____

_____

_____

_____

_____

Chapter 6
Sis, Don't Leave Them Debt, Leave Them Wealth

Understanding The Role Of Life
Insurance In Building

Imagine a family standing in the front pew of a church, dressed in black. The choir is singing softly, and the preacher's voice trembles as he says, "She was a good woman. She loved her family."

She did. She was.

But after the service, whispers start floating through the sanctuary.

"Who's covering the funeral?"

"Did she have insurance?"

"Nah, they're doing a GoFundMe."

This, happens in our community far too often. A woman who gave her whole life to others by raising children, caring for parents, and working two jobs, passes away leaving the family scrambling. People cook casseroles, pass around offering plates, and post links online just to give her a proper homegoing.

Let's be honest. Love doesn't pay for funerals. Dedication doesn't cover rent. Hard work alone doesn't guarantee security.

And what's worse? The emotional pain turns into financial chaos. I've seen siblings fight over funeral costs. I've seen children empty their savings to pay for caskets. I've seen children inherit more bills than memories.

We say, "She took care of everybody." If she didn't have insurance, that means nobody took care of her final chapter.

Let's flip the story.

Imagine another woman who was the same age, same faith, same love for her family. The difference is, this one had a plan. She sat down years before, got a policy, wrote out her wishes, and made sure her people knew where the paperwork was. When she passed, her family still cried, but they didn't crumble. Her children called the insurance company, filed a claim, and within weeks the funeral was paid for. Her home was paid off. Her grandchildren's college fund received a deposit.

That's not luck. That's legacy.

Now, let me tell you about a woman I actually met. She was 62, soft-spoken, and had raised three children on her own. She told me, "Janean, I've never been afraid to work. I am afraid to leave my children with nothing." She had just lost a close friend who died suddenly without insurance. The friend's children had to take out loans for the burial and move out of their mother's home because they couldn't afford the mortgage. After telling me the story, she described, "It just wasn't right," she said. "That's when I decided love isn't enough. I needed to leave protection."

She bought a $500,000 term life policy for less than $60 a month. Five years later, she passed away unexpectedly. Her oldest son called to say, "Mama made sure we were ok." That one decision...that $60 a month...changed her family's entire trajectory.

A hard truth is, you can't build generational wealth if you don't protect what you've already built. You can't say you're "breaking generational curses" if your family still has to beg strangers to bury you. Love your family enough to plan for them. Love them enough not to leave them struggling. Love without preparation leaves pain.

Life Insurance Is Not Morbid, It's Smart

We don't like to talk about death, especially in our community. In our families, it's taboo. We'll say things like, "Don't speak that over me," or "I'm not claiming that." We'll plan birthday parties a year in advance, we'll plan weddings a year in advance, but not a legacy plan for our families. We will organize every detail of a wedding, baby shower, or graduation party... Still, we will not plan a single detail about what happens when we're gone.

We don't want to face it because we associate life insurance with loss. Life insurance isn't about dying, it's about living well, even when you're gone. Yes, you might say, "I'm covered by faith." Let's be 100% honest, faith does not pay bills. While faith can move mountains, life insurance pays for funerals.

This chapter is not about fear; it's about protection.

It's not about death; it's about dignity.

Let's unpack why life insurance isn't just smart, it's essential.

1. **Life Insurance Is A Love Letter You Leave Behind**

    When my grandmother passed, she didn't leave a note. She left a plan. She had her policies, her will, and even a handwritten note in her Bible with the phone number of her insurance agent. That was her love letter. It wasn't words, it was wisdom.

That's what life insurance is. It's a final love note that says, "You can cry, but you don't have to struggle."

It even says, "Even if I'm gone, I've still got you."

It's not about money, it's about meaning. It's about ensuring the people you love can focus on healing instead of hustling. When you think of it that way, how could you not have a plan?

2. We Can't Build Wealth If We Keep Starting Over

Every time a loved one passes without coverage, the next generation has to start from scratch. They empty their savings, take out loans, or sell what little they have to cover final expenses. Then, when it's their time, the cycle repeats.

This repetition is one of the things that keeps our community stuck. We don't pass down assets; we pass down expenses and debt!

It's not because we don't care, it's because we were never taught. Many of our parents and grandparents didn't have access to the same information or opportunities. Some distrusted the system (rightfully so, after decades of predatory practices closed). Some simply didn't know where to start. You? You know better now. And when you know better, you do better.

We can't keep talking about "generational wealth" without first addressing "generational protection." You can't build on top of instability. Life insurance is the foundation. It's what makes sure your children's first step in life isn't backward.

3. Faith and Finances Go Together

Let's be honest, sometimes we confuse faith with avoidance. We say, "God will provide," but the truth is, God already did...through wisdom and opportunity.

Life insurance isn't a lack of faith; it's an act of faith. It's saying, "I trust God enough to use the tools he's given me." Scripture says, "a good man leaves an inheritance to his children's children." That's not just money...that's peace, property, and protection. In today's world, inheritance starts with something as simple as a policy.

I've heard people say, "I don't want to think about dying." I remind them, you're not planning for death, you're planning for dignity. It's not morbid to prepare; it's irresponsible not to.

4. Life Insurance Buys Time...And Time Is Priceless

Think about the moments right after someone passes. Bills don't pause. Rent doesn't wait. Credit card companies don't care if you're grieving.

Life insurance gives your family time...time to think, time to breathe, time to figure out the next step. That time is invaluable. Without it, people rush to make choices they regret. They sell the house too soon, move out of stability, or go back to work before they're emotionally ready. I once counseled a family who lost their matriarch. She didn't have insurance, and the daughter said something that I'll never forget: "I didn't even get to grieve my mama. I was too busy trying to pay for her."

No one should have to grieve and go broke at the same time. That's yet another benefit of having a policy. It gives your loved ones the gift of peace.

5. Life Insurance Bills Wealth Quietly

Here's what wealthy families understand that many of us don't: life insurance isn't just for emergencies, it's for elevation.

They use policies strategically:

- To start businesses
- To pay off mortgages
- To pay estate taxes
- To seed generational investments

It's not just a safety net, it's a launchpad.

And with modern policy options, life insurance can benefit you while you're still alive.

Whole Life policies grow cash value that you can borrow against tax free.

Indexed Universal Life (IUL) policies allow your money to grow alongside the market, building wealth without high risk.

Final Expense policies can ensure your family doesn't spend a single dime on your farewell.

In other words, life insurance isn't about preparing for the end. It's about creating a softer landing for the people you love and a stronger start for the ones coming after you.

6. Let's Talk About Myths

I've heard every excuse in the book, and I've said some of them myself once upon a time. Let's debunk them one by one.

Myth 1: "It's too expensive."
Truth: A healthy 30-year-old can get $250,000 of coverage for $25 to $30 a month. That's less than your streaming subscriptions combined.

Myth 2: "I don't need insurance because my job provides it."
Truth: Employer insurance is temporary. Once you retire, quit, or get laid off, that coverage ends. Personal insurance goes wherever you go.

Myth 3: "I'm too young to need that."
Truth: The younger and healthier you are, the cheaper it is. Waiting only costs more.

Myth 4: "I don't have kids."
Truth: Life insurance isn't just for parents...it's for anyone who doesn't want to leave debt behind. It can cover your parents, siblings, or whoever would carry your financial load.

Myth 5: "My family can just figure it out."
Truth: That's not love, that's leaving them in chaos.

We need to stop glorifying the struggle and start normalizing the plan.

7. Breaking the Silence

In many families, we don't talk about money, especially not about what happens after we're gone. We whisper about it, we joke about it, but we don't plan for it.

That silence keeps us trapped. It keeps us reactive instead of proactive.

We need to start having legacy conversations with the same energy we bring to baby showers, cookouts, and family reunions. Make it a tradition: "Everybody bring a dish...and your insurance paperwork."

Laugh about it if you must but normalize it. Every time you speak about money openly, you decrease the power the fear has.

8. Life Insurance As A Confidence Builder

Here's what people don't realize: getting insured isn't about protecting others, it changes *you*. It gives you a sense of security that spills into every other part of your life.

You stop living paycheck to paycheck in fear.

You start making decisions from a place of peace, not panic.

You start seeing yourself as a provider, a protector, and a legacy maker.

That confidence? That's wealth energy.

You can't truly financially feel free if you are still haunted by "what ifs." Life insurance quiets the "what ifs." It replaces them with, "even if."

"Even if something happens today, my people will be ok."

"Even if life takes a turn, my legacy will stand."

That's peace money can buy...and it's worth every cent.

9. The Emotional Weight Of Not Being Prepared

I've sat across from too many families in pain not just from loss, but from regret.

The regret of not having the conversation sooner.

The regret of ignoring the signs.

The regret of saying, "I'll do it next year."

And behind that regret is always love. They loved deeply, they just didn't prepare. Preparation is love. It's protection. It's emotional insurance for your family's peace of mind. When we're gone, the only thing they'll remember is whether we made it easier or harder for them to carry on.

10. The Legacy Equation

Here's the real equation of wealth:

Faith + Foresight + Financial Planning = Freedom

Faith without foresight is fragile. Foresight without a plan is fantasy. But when you put all three together, that's legacy.

Your life insurance policy is the first visit into your family's generational wealth account. It's how you start the chain reaction of financial security that can echo for decades.

It's your way of saying, "The struggle ends with me."

Takeaway

Sis, love without preparation leaves pain. You can't claim legacy if you're still leaving your family liability. Planning isn't morbid, it's mature. It's the highest form of love, the kind that keeps giving long after you're gone.

Too many of us are praying for generational wealth while avoiding the very tools that build it. We celebrate life loudly but prepare for loss silently, and that silence keeps our families struggling. Not you. Not anymore! You're choosing peace over panic, legacy over loss, and foresight over fear.

Life insurance isn't just paperwork. It's protection. It's power. It's a promise that even when you're gone, your love will still provide. That's what real wealth feels like...peace, provision, and pride in knowing your people are covered.

You are not planning for death, you are planning for dignity. You are securing futures. You are shifting your family's story from "they had to start over" to "she set us up right." The day you decide to protect what you've built is the day your legacy begins.

Say it with me:
- "I do not leave confusion. I leave clarity."
- "I do not leave debt. I leave direction."
- "I do not leave struggle. I leave strength."
- "My foresight is my family's freedom."

Affirm this truth, "My preparation is love in motion. My

planning is peace in advance. I am the bridge between my ancestors' prayers and my descendants' prosperity. My legacy will stand, because I cared enough to plan."

When you protect your life, you protect your lineage. The policy isn't the end...it's the foundation. You're not just ensuring your exit; you're insuring their elevation. This is how cycles break and legacies begin by making one wise, loving choice at a time.

Quick Exercise:
The Legacy Love Letter

If I'm not here tomorrow, what financial chaos would your loved ones have to face?

_____

_____

_____

_____

_____

_____

Who in my family would be the most affected, and how can I make the transition easier for them?

_____

_____

_____

_____

_____

_____

Is my current life insurance enough to protect my family's life-style, not just my funeral?

_____

_____

_____

_____

_____

_____

What would my love letter look like if I left one today?

_____

_____

_____

_____

_____

_____

Chapter 7
Sis, Put It In Writing – Wills, Trusts, & The Power of Planning

The Importance of Planning Your
Will and Trust

The sun has barely set after the funeral, but the family group chat is already in disarray.

"Auntie said the house was supposed to go to me."

"Girl, she told me the same thing!"

"Why is her boyfriend still staying there?"

Tension fills the air. The kitchen still smells like baked chicken and macaroni and cheese, but nobody's hungry anymore. Old memories mixed with new resentment. Someone finally says what everyone is thinking.

"Did she have a will?"

Silence.

That silence says it all.

Now it's lawyers, probate court, and property appraisals. Family members who once sat side by side in church won't even speak at reunions. All because nobody wrote it down. we say things like, "My kids know what I want," not taking into consideration grief makes people remember selectively. What feels like love to you can turn into confusion for them.

A will isn't about control...it's about care.

A trust isn't about greed...it's about guidance.

If you don't make a plan, the courts will...and the courts don't love your people the way you do.

I've seen it play out too many times. Someone dies without paperwork, and suddenly their life's work becomes a battleground. The house turns into a lawsuit. The bank account gets frozen. Cousins who once played double-dutch together now sit on opposite sides of a courtroom.

Sis, love your family enough to protect them from that kind of pain.

Death isn't the problem, disorganization is.

We don't talk about this enough because we've been taught to treat the subject like a curse. You say "will," and someone says, "Don't speak that over me." You say "trust," and someone else says, "That's for rich people."

Let's break both lies right now.

1. **You Don't Need Millions To Make A Plan**

    You don't need an estate the size of Oprah's to deserve order. If you've got *something* be it a house, a car, a savings account, your grandma's jewelry, a business, or children, you need a will.

    According to a 2024 Caring.com study, only 27% of Black adults have a will. The top reasons:

- "I don't have enough assets."
- "It's too expensive."
- "I don't know how."

    Here's what people don't realize, dying without a will costs more. Probate fees, court costs, legal delays, missed mortgage payments, frozen bank accounts. Your family could lose thousands just trying to claim what's rightfully theirs.

    Even worse, the state decides who gets what. That means strangers, not you, determine how your assets are split and who gets guardianship of your children.

Let that sink in. The law will decide who raises your babies if you don't.

2. The Emotional Price Of Silence

I met three sisters once who didn't speak for over a year after their father's death. They were fighting over his 20-year-old truck. It wasn't about the truck. It was about who mattered most.

Each wanted to feel chosen.

That's what happens when love isn't documented.

Silence creates suspicion. Suspicion breeds conflict.

You think you're keeping the peace by avoiding the topic. However, silence doesn't protect peace, it just delays pain.

3. A Will is Your Final Voice

A will isn't a legal maze. It's your voice on paper. It says:

- Here's who I trust to handle my affairs.
- Here's who I want to receive what.
- Here's how I want to be remembered.
- Here's who I want to raise my children.

Without it, judges, creditors, and sometimes even distant relatives decide for you.

Get it out of your head that by writing a will you are talking about death. You are really saying, "I love you enough to make this easier."

4. A Trust Is Your Financial Bodyguard

If a will says what happens after you pass, a trust controls what happens while you're still alive and after. It keeps things private, avoids probate court, and ensures your money, property, or investments go to the right people on the right timeline. You can even create conditions such as requiring your child to graduate college before accessing funds or leaving a portion to charity.

Wealthy families have been doing this forever. That's why their kids don't start from zero...they start from strategy.

5. Planning Isn't Morbid... It's Mature

We plan weddings down to the flower color. We plan vacations six months ahead. We plan baby showers, birthday parties, and brunches.

But we don't plan for what happens to the things and people we love most.

Sis, preparation doesn't attract death, it protects dignity. It says, "Even in my absence, I'm still in control of what I built." That is love with foresight.

Janean's Story: The Purple Folder That Saved A Family

I'll never forget Denise. She was a 58-year-old high school counselor who walked into my branch one spring afternoon with a purple folder tucked under her arm. She smiled and said, "Miss Janean, this right here is my peace." I was very curious as to what she meant by that. I soon found out.

Inside that folder:

- Her will
- Her life insurance policy
- Her mortgage deed
- Her passwords
- Her burial wishes
- Her kids' contact information

She said, "I told my children where it is. When my time comes, they'll know exactly what to do."

Two years later, Denise passed from a sudden stroke. Her daughter came into the branch, holding that same purple folder. There were tears, yes, but no chaos. No confusion. No fighting.

That folder became a family heirloom not because of what was in it, but because of what it prevented.

That's what planning does. It brings order where chaos could have been. It brings unity where confusion would have lived. It brings peace where panic usually shows up.

Practical Steps: How To Protect What You've Built

Now that we have faced the fear, let's walk through how to actually handle this like the boss you are.

Step 1: Take Inventory

Make a list of everything you own...and yes, everything counts.

- Homes, land, cars, jewelry, art
- Bank accounts and investment accounts
- 401(K)s, IRAs, and pensions
- Business ownership or side hustles
- Digital assets: social media, websites, crypto wallets
- Life insurance policies

If you can touch it, transfer it, or log into it, put it on the list. This list becomes your map. Without it, your family will spend months searching for things you could have listed in a single afternoon.

Step 2: Choose The Right People

Pick the right people for the right roles:

- _Executor_ – handles your estate after death
- _Guardian_ – cares for your children or dependents
- _Beneficiary_ – receives your property, money, or assets

Don't just pick your oldest child or closest cousin. Pick the most responsible person. The one who follows through, not the one who talks the loudest.

Step 3: Write Your Will

You can start simple.

Use resources like FreeWill.com, Trust & Will, or Legal-Zoom. Or hire a local attorney, most will draft a basic will for under $400.

Make sure:

- It's signed and dated.
- It has witnesses (per your state's laws).
- You keep the original in a safe place.

And for heaven's sake, tell somebody where it is.

Step 4: Create A Living Trust

If you own a home, run a business, or want privacy, a revocable living trust is gold. It keeps your estate out of probate (that's court), which can take 6-18 months and cost up to 5% of your estate's value.

You can even set up a trust that releases money gradually, protects monitors, or shields assets from certain taxes.

Step 5: Build A Legacy Binder

This is your "purple folder." Include:

- Will and trust documents
- Life insurance policies
- Birth and marriage certificates
- Deeds and car titles
- Account numbers and passwords
- A short letter to your loved ones (yes, really...say what you heart wants to say)

Keep it in a fireproof box, digital vault, or safety deposit box, and tell one trusted person where to find it.

Step 6: Review & Update

Every time life changes such as marriage, divorce, new baby, new property, etc., update your documents. Outdated instructions cause just as much confusion as no plan at all.

Step 7: Have The Conversation

Gather your people. Yes, even the ones who avoid hard talks. Cook a meal. Then tell them, "Listen, y'all. I've got something important to share. Here's my plan."

Tell them where the documents are, who's in charge, and why you made your choices. Transparency prevents tension later.

The Woman Who Waited Too Long

Let me tell you about Tasha. She was 44, a single mom of two teens, a nice townhouse, and a job with benefits. She always said, "I'll get my will done next year." Next year never came.

She was in a car accident.

She survived, thank God, but spent three weeks in the hospital. During that time, her bills piled up, her sister struggled to keep up with her kids' school paperwork, and nobody knew how to access her bank accounts.

When she recovered, the first thing she did was write her will. She told me, "I realized I don't have to die for my family to be lost. They were lost when I couldn't speak for myself."

That's what people miss; wills and trusts aren't just for the dead. They are for the living, too.

The Emotional Side: Peace In Preparation

Let's talk about how it feels to have your affairs in order.

It feels like taking a deep breath after holding it for years.

It feels like exhaling tension you didn't even realize you've been carrying.

It feels like quiet power...not loud, not flashy, but steady and sacred.

When your paperwork is done, when your people know where to find what they need, you start sleeping differently. The 2:00 a.m. "what if" thoughts fade. The low hum of anxiety that used to sit in the back of your mind quiets down.

You move differently, too.

You stop apologizing for being organized. You stop feeling guilty for talking about things people avoid. You stop carrying the invisible weight of *what would happen if*...because you already know the answer.

That confidence is a quiet luxury we don't talk about enough. It's the same feeling you get when your house is clean, your bills are paid, your gas tank is full, and your fridge is stocked except this time, the peace doesn't last for the weekend. It lasts for generations.

And there's something else, a calm that shows up in how you love. You love deeper when you're not distracted by fear. You show up more presently because you know you've handled your business. You feel proud of yourself not just for surviving, but for stewarding what you've built.

When I've seen women complete their plans including wills, trusts, insurance, and legacy binders, they always say the same thing, "I didn't know this would make me feel so free."

That's the beauty of preparation. It's not just about what happens after you're gone, it's about how you live while you're here. Peace and preparation is knowing that nothing you worked for will go to waste. It's knowing that your name will be attached to order, not mess. It's knowing your love is loud enough to echo long after you're gone.

Takeaway

Sis, avoiding the conversation doesn't stop the inevitable, it only shifts the burden. Love without a plan becomes confusion. Effort without a will becomes chaos...a word you've heard several times throughout this book. Silence, no matter how gentle, still leaves scars.

You've worked too hard to leave your life open to

interpretation. Putting it in writing is your final act of leadership.

Say it with me:

- "I choose clarity over confusion."
- "I am my family's peacekeeper."
- "I organized my life because my love deserves order."
- "My legacy will not be left to chance."

Affirm this truth, "My preparation is my protection. My paperwork is my power. My love is structured, documented, and deliberate. I will not leave confusion, I will leave clarity, dignity, and direction."

One day, when your family opens that folder, whatever color it is, they won't just find papers. They'll find proof that you love them enough to plan.

Quick Exercise:
Legacy and Legal Clarity

Ask yourself...

Who knows where my documents are?

_____

_____

_____

_____

_____

_____

Who would pay my bills if I couldn't?

_____

_____

_____

_____

_____

_____

Who would raise my children if I passed tomorrow?

_____

_____

_____

_____

_____

_____

If you don't have clear answers, it's time to write them.

Chapter 8
Sis, Protect Your Peace And Your Purse

The Value of a Prenuptial or Post-nuptial Agreement, Regardless of Asset Size

Picture wo women are sitting at brunch. One is newly engaged, hand flashing her ring every few seconds. The other is recently divorced, no ring anymore, just lessons. The conversation shifts from the wedding venue to the guest list to the dress. The newly engaged friend says, "He mentioned something about a prenup, but I told him that's for people with real money."

The table goes quiet. The divorced friend just swirls her mimosa and smiles a half-sad, half-wise smile that only experience can teach.

She says softly, "I used to think the same thing. But sis, I wish I'd signed one."

Her friend looks confused. "You didn't have millions, though."

"No," she says, "but I had peace. I had a business. I had savings. And I lost all of it because we didn't have boundaries on paper."

She goes on to explain how her small catering business, the one she built from scratch before the marriage, was considered a marital asset. How the divorce attorney fees cost more than the wedding did. How the house they bought together went to him because his name was on the loan even though she paid half of the bills.

"Don't get me wrong, I loved that man. However, love without clarity gets expensive."

That's the part most of us don't talk about. We'll spend thousands on our wedding, but not a dime on protection. We'll pray for "forever" without planning for if forever ends. Not because we expect it to, but because maturity means preparing for all outcomes, even the ones our hearts don't want to imagine.

A prenup (before marriage) or postnup (after marriage) isn't an act of mistrust. It's an act of love with boundaries. It says, "I respect you enough to be transparent." It says, "I'm here for partnership, not ownership." It says, "We both matter, and so does the work we've done before we met."

Truthfully, marriage is more than romance. It's a merger. And no smart woman signs a business contract without reading the fine print.

Why Protection Is Power

Let's reframe this right now.

A prenuptial agreement isn't about expecting divorce, it's about expecting accountability. It's not "planning to fail," it's planning to protect what you've worked hard for, no matter what happens.

We've been conditioned to think a prenup is cold, transactional, or unromantic. The reality is that clarity is love. Confusion causes conflict. The clearer your financial expectations are before and during the marriage, the fewer arguments, misunderstandings, and regrets you'll face later.

Money is one of the top reasons marriages end. Money. And it's not always because people are greedy, it's because people make assumptions. "I thought you'd handle that bill." "I thought we were saving together." "I thought your debt didn't matter once we got married."

Here's what a prenup or postnup really says:

"We both bring value to this relationship."

"We both have something to protect, emotionally and financially."

"We're building something together, but we're not erasing what came before us."

That matters for every woman, regardless of income. Maybe you don't have a mansion or a million-dollar portfolio. But do you have a savings account? A 401(k)? A small business? Even a family home your grandmother left you? Then, you have something worth protecting.

The moment you say, "I do," those lines blur both legally and financially. Without a clear agreement, state laws decide who gets what. Not love. Not fairness. Not intention. The state. And baby, the state doesn't care about your late nights, your sacrifices, or your dreams.

Janean's Story: Love, Boundaries, And Lessons

By 2012, I had successfully built a career, established a comfortable home, and welcomed a beautiful child into the world. I had achieved a sense of stability that many would envy, yet there was still one crucial element missing from the picture: I didn't have a husband. Soon, to merely tick the final item off my mental checklist, I found myself in my first marriage.

As I pondered my feelings, I realized that I wasn't entirely sure if I truly loved him. What I loved was the idea of marrying someone—of finally fulfilling that long-held dream of walking down the aisle. This realization became my truth. At 42 years old, I felt the pressure of time weighing on me. Society often places a timeline on personal milestones, and I could feel the urgency creeping in. I thought getting married would somehow validate my accomplishments and solidify my sense of belonging.

In the midst of planning the wedding, I found myself dismissing the importance of a prenuptial agreement. I had assets that I should have considered protecting, but my focus was firmly fixed on the excitement of the wedding day rather than the realities of the commitment itself. I was swept up in the romance and the fairy tale of it all, failing to acknowledge the potential risks that come with any union.

As it turned out, the marriage was short-lived and, to my dismay, lasted a mere twelve months. During the divorce proceedings, I was taken aback when my husband had the audacity to ask for spousal support. I was floored by his request; it felt like a betrayal of the very foundation we had supposedly built together. This experience, however, turned out to be a significant learning lesson for me. I came to understand that protection and clarity are essential components to achieving peace in any relationship.

Looking back, I realize that I should have taken the time

to consider not just the romantic aspects of marriage but also the practical implications. The lessons learned from that tumultuous experience have shaped my perspective on love, commitment, and the importance of safeguarding oneself in relationships. Now, I approach such matters with a newfound appreciation for the balance between emotional connection and practical foresight.

The Cultural Conversation: Breaking The Stigma

Let's address the elephant in the room, the stigma around prenups in our community. We whisper about them like they're curses. "She doesn't trust her man." "He must have something to hide." "They must be planning to break up."

Sis, we have to do better.

We ensure everything else like our phones, our cars, our homes, even our jewelry. Yet, we refuse to ensure our lives' biggest financial partnership: marriage.

A prenup doesn't mean you love your partner less. It means you love yourself enough not to lose you in the process. It means you love them enough to help prevent resentment later.

See yourself the same way the wealthy families do, most wealthy families don't see prenups as optional. They see them as protection for both parties. They know that fair doesn't happen by accident, it happens by agreement.

We have to unlearn the belief that security and romance can't coexist. They can. In fact, the healthiest relationships are the ones where transparency, honesty, and fairness live right along with affection, loyalty, and interest.

The Practical Side: What Prenups And Postnups Actually Do

Now, let's make this plain. Here's what a well-written prenup or postnup can cover.

1. **Protect personal assets.** Anything you owned before marriage such as your business, inheritance, savings, or property, stays yours. It's not about being selfish; it's about being smart.

    Think about it like this, if you bought your home before marriage, that's your roof. You maintain it, you insure it, and you keep it in your name. That's not to exclude your partner, but to protect what you've already built. The same goes for your creative work, your intellectual property, your side hustles, and even the savings account your mama told you to keep "just in case."

    A good agreement draws that line clearly. What's yours before the marriage should stay yours, not by secrecy but by structure.

2. **Define marital assets.** It clarifies what's "ours" versus

"mine." That's how you avoid confusion, especially when it comes to income, real estate, or investments. This is where you and your partner create financial boundaries together.

A prenup or postnup lets you decide how to handle shared purchases from joint bank accounts to vehicles to the dream house you'll buy down the line. It ensures there is no confusion about who contributed what and how those contributions will be treated if the marriage ends or if one partner passes away.

Clarity is what prevents bitterness later. It lets both of you feel safe knowing that no one will walk away empty-handed or overburdened. "Ours" should never mean "yours disappears."

3. **Safeguard from debt.** If your partner has existing debt, a prenup can protect you from being legally responsible for it. (And vice versa.)

   This is one of the most overlooked reasons for these agreements. Love might make you blind, but debt will make you see real quick, lol! Without a prenup, if your spouse has unpaid credit cards, tax liens, student loans, or business losses, they could legally become your problem.

   You might not have swiped that card or signed for that loan, but if you don't protect yourself, you might still end up paying for it. A clear prenup or postnup says, "Will share life, not liabilities."

4. **Protect your children.** If you have kids from a previous relationship, a prenup can ensure their inheritance isn't accidentally mixed into marital property.

That's a big one, especially for women who've already built something before remarrying or want to leave specific assets to their children. Without this kind of planning, those assets can get tangled up in probate court, leaving your kids to fight for what's rightfully theirs.

A well-drafted prenup (or postnup) clearly names your children and designates the assets meant for them such as your home, life insurance, retirement funds, or even sentimental things like jewelry or family land. You're saying, "My love is big enough for everyone, and my planning makes sure nobody gets left out."

5. **Outline financial roles.** Who pays which bills? Who handles which accounts? Clarity avoids resentment. One of the biggest causes of friction in marriage isn't how much money there is, it's how the money is handled. Without an agreement, assumptions turn into arguments.

   A prenup or postnup helps set expectations early. You might decide that one partner gets the mortgage while the other covers household expenses or that joint savings will go toward travel or retirement. These conversations don't kill romance, they create teamwork.

   When you know your role and your partner knows theirs, nobody feels taken advantage of. Everyone knows the playbook, and you both win.

6. **Define spousal support.** It can establish fair expectations for alimony, depending on contributions and lifestyle.

   Here's why that matters...marriages end for all

kinds of reasons, but the financial fallout doesn't have to be devastating. This section allows both partners to agree on what's fair before emotions or lawyers get involved.

It can ensure that a stay-at-home spouse who sacrifices a career for the family is treated with fairness just as it can protect an entrepreneur who took all the financial risk in building a business.

It's not about predicting separation; it's about protecting equity, both emotional and financial. You're saying, "If life happens, we'll handle it with grace, not greed."

7. **Protect future earnings.** If you're an entrepreneur, artist, or professional with growing potential, it ensures your future value isn't automatically up for grabs.

    That matters because sometimes your biggest success comes after marriage...the book deal, the promotion, the business boom. Without an agreement, your spouse could legally have claim to part of it, even if they weren't part of the grind that got you there.

    A prenup or postnup makes sure your future wins are respected, while still allowing you to share what you choose to share. It lets you protect your potential while still being generous with your partnership. Love should never cost your legacy.

    That's not pessimism that's planning.

The Emotional Side: How Protection Creates Peace

I've had women tell me, "Janean, I feel guilty even thinking about this. It feels like I'm planning for the worst."

I get it.

However, let me offer another perspective. It's not about expecting the worst, it's about expecting yourself to stay whole no matter what. When you have legal and financial protection in place, you can love freely. You can show up fully. Because you're not scared of losing yourself in someone else's dream.

Let's look at it this way, a prenup or postnup removes fear from the foundation. It says, "We both know who we are and what we're bringing to this table.

And that piece? That's priceless.

Nothing feels better than knowing you can choose to stay not because you *have* to, but because you *want* to.

Takeaway

Sis, let's be real, love is beautiful, but it's not blind. You can hold someone's heart and still hold on to your head. You can be romantic and responsible. You can pray for "forever" and still prepare for "just in case." That's not fear. That's foresight. That's wisdom dressed in heels.

For too long, we've been taught that asking questions about money and marriage means we don't just trust our partners. What if it really means we're learning to trust ourselves? A prenup or postnup isn't a prediction of failure. It's a declaration of self-respect. It's saying, "I know who I am, I know what I've worked for, and I know that love doesn't require me to forget either."

When you protect your assets, you're not protecting just numbers, you're protecting years of sacrifice. Every late night you worked. Every "I'll wait until payday." Every dream you turned into dollars. Every boundary you had to build. You are safeguarding your history so you can write your future freely.

Let's talk about peace for a second.

Peace hits differently when your name is on your business and your balance sheet. Peace is loving fully because you're not secretly afraid of losing everything if the relationship shifts. Peace is signing papers with pride because you know what's yours and what's shared. Peace is not having to choose between your heart and your hard-earned stability.

So many women have walked through divorce or separation with confusion and regret, not because they didn't love deeply, but because they didn't plan wisely. We don't talk enough about how grief feels when it's mixed with debt. We don't talk about how harassment creeps in when your name is on loans you didn't make or when your business becomes collateral for someone else's decisions.

That ends with you. You're not repeating that story. You are rewriting it.

You're building a partnership rooted in truth. You're walking into relationships as a whole woman, emotionally available but financially aware. True intimacy isn't just pillow talk. It's paperwork talk. It's asking, "What's your credit score?" with the same confidence you ask, "What's your love language?"

A healthy relationship isn't built on fantasy, it's built on transparency. You don't need matching hoodies and social media posts to prove your love; you need matching goals and mutual respect. That's real alignment. And let's be clear, having a prenup or postnup doesn't mean you expect to walk away. It means you expect both of you to grow, evolve, and protect the foundation you're building together.

You deserve a love that's both tender and trans-parent. You deserve a partnership that honors not only your emotions but also your efforts. You deserve the freedom to love without fear or financial fallout.

Clarity is sexy.

Stability is seductive.

Accountability is attractive.

When two grown people sit down and say, "Let's make sure we are both protected," that's not cold, that's commitment.

Say it with me:

- "I protect what I build."
- "I lead with love, but I'm not afraid of logic."
- "My boundaries are not barriers, they are bridges to peace."
- "My partnership will be rooted in transparency, trust, and teamwork."

Affirm this truth, "I am worthy of love that respects my value, honors my effort, and protects my legacy. My security does not shrink my softness. My wisdom does not weaken my worth. I am both romance and reason, and that balance is my superpower."

Love without clarity costs too much, and you've already paid your dues.

Quick Exercise:
The "If Something Happens" Test

Answer these questions honestly.

What do I own or earn right now that I want protected if I got married?

_____

_____

_____

_____

_____

_____

What financial habits or debts would I bring into a relationship?

_____

_____

_____

_____

_____

_____

If I divorced tomorrow, what would I regret not having protected?

_____

_____

_____

_____

_____

_____

What does fairness look like to me in partnership?

_____

_____

_____

_____

_____

_____

What conversation have I been avoiding about money and marriage, and who do I need to have it with?

_____

_____

_____

_____

_____

Bonus Challenge: Write Your Partnership Vision Statement

Describe what healthy financial love looks like to you. What does teamwork, transparency, and respect sound like in your future household?

_____

_____

_____

_____

_____

_____

_____

_____

_____

_____

_____

_____

_____

_____

_____

Chapter 9
Sis, Don't Just Dream It, Do It

Designing a Vision Board to
Represent Your Financial Goals

L et's envision the scene. It is early January. Your living room smells like a fresh candle; vanilla and possibility. The table is covered with magazines, scissors, glue sticks, and your dreams. Your playlist is vibing, and you've got your favorite drink nearby, maybe coffee, maybe champagne, depending on your mood.

You're ready. You start cutting out words like freedom, travel, paid in full, abundance, and peace. You feel the energy of it all...fresh year, new beginnings, clean slate.

Halfway through, something clicks. You realize your board looks more like an aesthetic mood collage than a plan for your real life. It's got beaches and handbags and brunches. Yet, there's not much about how to make those things possible.

Sis, that's where many of us lose the thread.

We dream big, but we plan small. We manifest feelings but forget frameworks.

A financial vision board bridges that gap. It doesn't just show what you want, it reflects what you're willing to work toward. You see, manifestation is only half the recipe. The other half is management. It's not enough to see the vision, you have to finance the vision.

When Vision Meets Reality

Let me tell you about "Tasha."

Tasha was the "vision board queen." Every January, she hosted her girlfriends for what she called her "vision and vibes brunch." There was champagne, music, and glitter everywhere on her board. Whew! It was a masterpiece. It had the word "boss" in bold gold letters, photos of tropical beaches, luxury cars, dream homes, and the word "freedom" front and center.

When December rolled back around, Tasha admitted something to me. "Janean, my boards always come out beautifully. Sadly, my bank account looks the same every year."

I asked her to bring her last vision board over. I studied it and smiled. "Sis, this board has everything you want but nothing tells you how you're going to get it."

She laughed, then sighed. "So you're saying I made a mood board, not a money board?"

Exactly.

See, the difference between a dreamer and a builder is in the details. A mood board shows what looks good. A financial vision board shows what's possible and how to get there.

We sat down together and reworked it.

- Instead of "travel more," she wrote:
  - ➢ "$150 per month into travel savings fund."
- Instead of "debt free life," she added:
  - ➢ "Pay off credit card balance by November 15th."
- Instead of "financial freedom," she wrote:
  - ➢ "Emergency fund: $3,000 saved."

The next year, her results looked different. She didn't just cross off goals, she became the woman on the board. Tasha learned that her board wasn't magic; it was management with visuals. It turned her wishes into measurable wins.

Why Visualization Works

Here's something both spiritual and scientific. Your brain doesn't just respond to effort; it responds to imagery.

Visualization activates the same part of your brain that fires when you perform an action. That means when you see yourself accomplishing something, your body starts to believe it can.

That's not wishful thinking, that's neuroscience.

A 2023 study from Dominion University of California found that people who write and visualize their goals are 42% more likely to achieve them than those who don't. Why? Because when your goals are visible, your choices subconsciously begin aligning with them.

You start making micro decisions that move you forward...skipping a splurge here, saving a little there, and investing instead of impulsively spending.

That's what your vision board does, it keeps your why's louder than your why not's.

Every time you walk past it, you're reminded of your purpose. You're reminded that your goals aren't random, they're sacred.

Your board becomes a mirror of the woman you're becoming, the one who's intentional with her time, her talent, and her treasure.

Building A Vision Board For Your Wallet

Let's go from concept to construction. A financial vision board isn't about perfection, it's about purpose. You don't need fancy supplies or expensive art, you need clarity and commitment.

Here is how to design a board that blends beauty with blueprint.

Step 1: Reflect Before You Cut

Before you pick up the scissors, pick up a pen. Ask yourself...

- What do I truly want for my life? Not just this year, but for the next 5 years?
- What financial habits have held me back?
- What kind of woman do I want to become? Disciplined? Debt free? Secure? Generous?

Write it all down. Clarity before creativity.

Step 2: Choose Your 5 Pillars

A good vision board has balance. Create five clear sections that will reflect your money goals.

1. **Earning:** Your job, your side hustle, or business goals. (example: "Launch Etsy store," "Negotiate salary increase," "Monetize my skill.")
2. **Saving:** Emergency funds, sinking funds, specific savings goals. ("Save $5,000 for emergencies by December 31st.")
3. **Debt Freedom:** Credit card payoff, student loans, car notes. ("Pay off Chase card... $3,200 remaining.")
4. **Investing:** Retirement, stocks, real estate, business equity. ("Max out 401(k) match," "Buy my first rental property.")
5. **Lifestyle and Legacy:** Travel, giving, family, home ownership, philanthropy. ("Open a scholarship fund for my niece," "Plan family reunion fund.")

Each pillar gets visuals and numbers to help manifestation, which needs math.

Step 3: Add Visual Anchors That Make You Feel Wealthy, Not Just Look It

Instead of only adding a mansion or a yacht, try this:

- A smiling woman checking her savings app.
- A "paid in full" statement.
- A check made out to yourself for your dream income.
- A quiet morning scene with the caption "peaceful and debt-free."

Choose images that evoke calm confidence, not

comparison.

Step 4: Get Specific with Numbers and Dates

Saying "save more" isn't specific enough. Instead, try…

- "Save $300 a month."
- "Reach $10,000 savings by next December."
- "Pay off $2,500 of debt in 10 months."

Specificity is the bridge between goals and results. Numbers hold you accountable.

Step 5: Speak Life with Financial Affirmations

The words on your board should speak to both your heart and your habits. Here are some powerful affirmations to include…

- "My bank account reflects my boundaries."
- "I manage my money with confidence and clarity."
- "Abundance flows because I plan and prepare."
- "My savings protects my peace."
- "I'm not afraid of numbers, they tell my story of growth."

These reminders help when your motivation fades and keep your energy focused.

Step 6: Keep it Visible and Update it Often

Your board shouldn't live in a closet. It should live where your habits live, which are above your desk, near your bed, or beside your mirror.

Look at it daily. Touch it weekly. Adjust it quarterly.

This isn't a night craft project, it's a living financial document. Add sticky notes when you reach milestones. Tape receipts from debt payments. Post bank screenshots when your savings grows.

Celebrate progress visibly. You're literally watching your wealth story unfold in real time.

Janean's Story: The Board That Shifted My Belief

I'll never forget the year I made my first finances-only vision board. No quotes about "living my best life." No beaches. No purses. Just numbers, affirmations, and receipts of progress.

One corner had "Debt-free December" written. Another said, "$1,000 emergency fund." I even printed my credit card statements, not to shame myself but to face them with power. Every morning, I'd glance at the board before work and whisper, "peace over panic." That simple ritual built a kind of quiet accountability. When I wanted to splurge, I thought about the board. When I paid off a balance, I taped the word "done" over it.

By the end of the year, not only was I debt-free, I was different. My money mindset shifted from avoidance to authority.

That's what I want for you. Not just a board full of dreams, a board that reflects a woman in control.

Seeing Your Future Before It Arrives

Let's be honest, sis, money is emotional. It's not just math on the spreadsheet; it's memories, fears, hopes, and proof of how we see ourselves. When you sit down to create a financial vision board, you're not just pasting dreams onto poster paper. You're piecing together parts of your future self...one intention, one image, and one affirmation at a time.

For many women, this process feels deeply personal. If you've ever struggled financially, every picture of peace and prosperity feels like a quiet rebellion. It's you saying, "I will not repeat the patterns that kept me struggling. I will not apologize for wanting more."

When you build your vision board with intention, you're not fantasizing, you are fortifying. You're training your mind to recognize abundance as familiar, not foreign. You're rewriting your internal story from "I hope I can" to "I know I will."

That, right there, is where transformation begins.

Visualization has power because it connects your emotions to your actions. When you see the life you desire, your spirit starts to believe it's already yours. You begin to walk differently, spend differently, and make decisions that align with that image. You start saying "no" to distractions because the woman on that board...the one who is debt-free, at peace, and purposeful...wouldn't waste her energy that way.

It's a sacred shift.

Your vision board becomes more than motivation; it becomes a mirror. A reflection of the woman you are becoming, not the one who doubts, the one who decides.

When you look at that board, you should see a story unfolding.

- The woman who stopped letting her past dictate her plans.
- The woman who turned budgeting into a love language with herself.
- The woman who no longer hustles for worthiness but builds from wisdom.

As the months go by, something subtle happens. You start noticing pieces of that board showing up in real life. The savings account balance that once felt impossible starts to grow. The side hustle you named in the corner suddenly becomes your main income stream. The peace you pictured starts living in your mornings.

Then, you have an epiphany. Your vision board isn't predicting your future, it's preparing you for it. It's emotional because you see evidence of healing. It's powerful because you're shown proof of growth. It's spiritual because your faith has turned tangible.

Don't rush this part. Light a candle, play some music, and let yourself feel it. Feel the gratitude for what's already on the way. Feel the pride for how far you've come. Feel the calm of knowing that financial freedom isn't just possible, it's personal. When you can see your future before it arrives, you start walking like it's already here. And that confidence? That's the currency that changes everything.

Takeaway

Your financial vision board is more than a collage; it's a contract between your present and your future. It's you promising yourself that the life you want isn't too big, too bold, or too far away. It's you saying, "I'm done just surviving, I'm designing."

We often underestimate the power of seeing our goals daily. Here's the truth: the more your eyes witness abundance, the more your mind believes it, and the more your actions align to match it. You start making better money choices not because someone told you to, but because your vision won't let you settle for less.

When you look at your board don't just see pictures, recognize them as reminders of who you are becoming:

- The woman who no longer apologizes for wanting nice things *and* a savings account.
- The woman who pays herself first and walks with her head high.
- The woman who is no longer afraid to say, "I deserve this, and I've planned for it."

Every image, every word, every number on that board

should speak to your next level. You're not building a fantasy, you're building focus. And focus builds freedom.

Remember faith without works is fantasy. You can't just pin pictures of luxury and expect wealth to land in your lap. You have to pair your board with budgeting, discipline, and follow through. Your board isn't a wish list; it's a work list. It's the visual accountability partner that whispers, "Keep going, girl. You said you wanted this."

When life tries to distract you, because you know it will, your board becomes your anchor. On days you're tired, when bills pile up, when progress feels slow. You can look at that vision and remember why you started. You'll see that every small choice, every "no" to impulse spending, every "yes" to saving and planning is pushing you closer to that woman staring back at you.

Your financial vision board is sacred ground. Treat it like an altar for your ambitions. A daily space where gratitude meets grind. Abundance doesn't arrive by accident. It shows up for women who stay consistent, intentional, and unafraid to imagine more.

Say it with me:

- "I see it, so I can become it."
- "My goals are not wishes, they are assignments."
- "Every picture I place is a prayer I'm preparing to answer."
- "I am not waiting for wealth to find me; I am walking toward it every day."

Affirm this truth, "I am the architect of my abundance. I am the designer of my destiny. My vision is clear, my steps are ordered, and my future is unfolding exactly as I've pictured it...full, free, and financially secure."

Your dreams are waiting for you to catch up. So, go ahead hang that vision board somewhere bold. Let it speak over you every single day. When you see things clearly, you can build what you see confidently.

Quick Exercise:
Money Map Vision

Answer these questions honestly.

What are my top three financial priorities for the next 12 months?

_____

_____

_____

_____

_____

What habits or distractions keep me from reaching them?

_____

_____

_____

_____

_____

What does financial peace look and feel like to me?

_____

_____

_____

_____

_____

_____

What images, numbers, or quotes could represent those goals visually?

_____

_____

_____

_____

_____

_____

What's one financial milestone I'll celebrate this quarter, and how?

_____

_____

_____

_____

_____

_____

Bonus Challenge: Create a "Progress Board" beside your vision board.

Use three columns labeled: Debt Down, Savings Up, Goals Met. Add visuals, receipts, or quotes each month to track your transformation.

You'll be surprised how powerful it feels to see your progress building one choice, one month, and one payment at a time.

Chapter 10
Sis, Peace Lives In The Plan

Creating a Comprehensive
Financial Checklist

H ere's another scenario. It's Saturday morning. The sun is peeking through your blinds, coffee is brewing, and you finally have a little peace before the day gets loud. You pull out your laptop to "check your balance real quick." You just want to make sure the bills went through and *boom*! Your chest tightens. You see three different automatic payments, two you forgot about, and one late fee that makes you question all your life choices.

You close the screen, take a deep breath, and whisper, "Lord, just give me strength."

Then, like most of us, you promise yourself, "Next month, I'm getting organized." However, next month comes with new chaos. The car needs tires, the kids need clothes, the fridge starts to hum like it's about to retire. And suddenly, "getting organized" gets pushed to "someday."

That "someday" moment is where most women live; halfway between good intentions and financial exhaustion.

Now, imagine instead of panic-checking your account on random Saturdays, you have a rhythm. A ritual. A system. Imagine sitting down once a month with a warm drink and a clear checklist. One that shows you exactly where your money's been, where it's going, and how close you are to your goals.

That's not stress. That is structure. That's peace you can measure.

I remember a client who I will call Monique. Brilliant and ambitious, working full-time and running a side hustle. She wasn't broke, but she was busy. Too busy to track the money she worked so hard for. She told me, "Janean, I make good money but I feel broke all the time."

We sat down together, and I walked her through what I call a "purse check." This is actually the same checklist you're about to create. Thirty minutes later, she knew exactly where her money was hiding...old subscriptions, duplicate apps, forgotten savings accounts, and late payments that were quietly bleeding her budget.

When we finished, she laughed and said, "You mean I've been losing peace over things I could fix in one lunch break?"

Exactly.

That's the checklist moment, the instant you realize your financial overwhelm wasn't because you're bad with money. It's because you were trying to remember everything instead of writing it down.

Sis, our brains weren't built to hold every password, bill, due date, and balance. That's what systems are for. You don't need to hustle harder, you need to hustle smarter.

That's what this chapter is about, turning mental clutter into money clarity. Peace doesn't come from having more, it comes from knowing exactly what you already have and what to do with it.

Why A Checklist Matters

Let's be real, a checklist doesn't sound glamorous. It's not flashy. It won't go viral. You can't wear it or post it. But it's one of the most powerful financial tools you'll ever create.

Here's why...

Without a checklist, money slips through the cracks quietly. You don't notice $12.99 here or $48.50 there until you're wondering why your balance doesn't match your hard work. When you use a checklist consistently, you bring your finances out of hiding. You make the invisible visible.

Think of a checklist as financial accountability in plain sight. It shows you what's real instead of what's assumed. It gives you data instead of drama. Think about it, if you can make a grocery list to feed your body, why wouldn't you make a financial list to feed your peace?

Women, especially, carry invisible mental spreadsheets every day...

- Did the rent hit?
- Did the car payment clear?
- Did I transfer the savings?
- Did I cancel that free trial before it turned into a charge?

That's not freedom, that's fatigue.

A financial checklist takes those spending thoughts and pins them to paper, where you can see them clearly and check them off with pride. Each check mark becomes a mini celebration of control unclaimed.

Let me sprinkle in a fact. According to a 2023 NerdWallet survey, 61% of Americans say financial uncertainty causes them daily stress while people who tracked their expenses and goals regularly reported significantly less anxiety and more confidence about the future. Why? Because clarity kills fear.

When you write down where your money is going, you

strip your money of misery. You stop reacting and start responding. You go from "I hope I'm ok" to "I know exactly where I stand." That confidence changes how you move through the world. You stop flinching at every notification. You stop avoiding mail. You start showing up in your financial life like a woman who knows her numbers, her goals, and her work.

What gets tracked gets transformed. Every empire started with a plan. Every stable household started with a structure. Every peaceful woman started with a list that kept her aligned when life tried to pull her off balance. That's what this checklist will do for you. Don't think of it as busy work, it's blueprint work. It's how you audit your habits, honor your progress, and hold yourself accountable. One line, one box, one "check" at a time.

Janean's Story: The Power Of Paper Proof

I'll never forget the first year I did my own financial audit. I had been working in banking for years, teaching others about budgeting, saving, and investing. My personal finances? They were decent, not disciplined.

One day, I sat at my kitchen table with a notebook, coffee, and determination. I listed every bill, every debt, every account, every goal. It took hours. By the end, I had five pages...and a headache. However when I looked at it, I felt something I hadn't felt in months, which was peace.

Instead of vague worry, I had data. Instead of stress, I had structure. I could finally see where I was bleeding, where I was blessed, and where I needed boundaries.

That night I made a promise to myself. I was not going to play anymore guessing games about my finances. Every quarter, I would check my progress. Every December, I would celebrate what I'd improved.

And that's exactly what I did. Within a year, I paid off two credit cards, boosted my savings, and started investing for real. The difference wasn't more income; it was more intention. That's what I want for you. Not perfection, but proof. Not shame, but strategy.

What Goes on a Comprehensive Financial Checklist

Think of your checklist like a purse inventory. You're dumping everything out, deciding what stays, what goes, and what needs organizing.

Here's what your checklist should cover and why each item matters.

1. **Income Review**
- Do you know exactly how much you earn monthly after taxes?
- Have you reviewed all sources of income including salary, side hustles, passive income, bonuses?
- Are there opportunities to increase your income

(negotiation, certification, business growth)?

Why it matters: If you don't track your inflow, you'll always underestimate your power and overestimate your problems. Income awareness builds confidence and creativity.

2. Expense Audit

- List every recurring bill (rent, utilities, subscriptions, insurance).
- Highlight silent spenders such as fees, impulse buys, or delivery apps.
- Cancel what doesn't add value.

Why it matters: You can't grow what you don't guard. An expense audit is like spring cleaning your wallet, it makes room for peace and profit.

3. Savings Checkpoint

- Do you have an emergency fund to cover at least three months of expenses?
- Are you contributing consistently to short-term and long-term savings?
- Is your money in an account that earns interest instead of dust?

Why it matters: Savings aren't about fear; they're about freedom. It's knowing that one unexpected bill can't break your peace.

4. Debt Dashboard

- List every debt: credit cards, student loans, car payments, mortgage, personal loans.
- Record the balance, interest rate, and minimum payment.
- Note any progress since your last review.

Why it matters: Debt doesn't define you, but ignoring it delays your destiny. Awareness is how you start shifting from survival payments to strategic payoffs.

5. Credit Check

- Know your credit score within 10 points.
- Review your credit report annually for errors.
- Set a goal for credit improvement (Example: raised score from 640 to 700).

Why it matters: Your credit score is your financial reputation. It's not about perfection; it's about progress. Every 10-point jump means more opportunity, less interest, and more options.

6. Insurance Inventory

- Health, auto, renters or homeowners, and life insurance.
- Are your policies current? Are the beneficiaries up-to-date?
- Do you have enough coverage to protect your family's future?

Why it matters: Protects your peace. You don't wait for the storm to buy an umbrella.

7. Retirement Review

- Are you contributing to your employer's retirement plan or your own IRA?
- Are you taking full advantage of employer matches?
- Do you know your projected retirement income versus need?

Why it matters: You can't retire on vibes. You need a vision. Every dollar you invest for tomorrow buys you time and dignity later.

8. Investment Snapshot

- What investments do you currently hold (stocks, ETF's, real estate, business equity)?
- Are they diversified, or are you overexposed in one area?
- Have you reviewed your risk tolerance recently?

Why it matters: Wealth grows where attention goes. Investing isn't gambling, it's gardening. Check what you've planted and prune what's not producing.

9. Legal and Legacy Documents

- Will, trust, power of attorney, health directive.
- Are they current? Does someone trusted know where they are?

- Do your beneficiaries reflect your present reality, not your past?

  Why it matters: Legacy isn't just what you leave behind; it's what you live with peace about.

10. Goals and Giving

- Are your financial goals written and measurable?
- Have you built giving into your budget like tides, charity, and community support?

  Why it matters: Generosity expands capacity. The more you give with wisdom, the more abundance flows through you.

Confidence Through Clarity

Let's talk about how it feels to be organized.

It feels lighter. It feels quieter in your spirit. It feels like you finally put your life on solid ground.

That's what financial order does, it settles your nervous system. You stop flinching at e-mail notifications. You stop avoiding your mail. You breathe easier knowing everything has a name, a place, and a plan.

Financial chaos drains confidence; clarity restores it.

Every check mark you make tells your inner critic, "I'm not stuck, I'm stewarding."

When you have your money mapped out, even surprises don't scare you. Flat tire? Covered. Sick day? Planned for. Job change? Adjusted. Because order doesn't eliminate life's challenges, it equips you to face them.

Takeaway

Sis, money maturity is measured by maintenance. You can't call it growth if you never check on it. The financial checklist doesn't make you controlling, it makes you conscious.

You can't fix what you won't face, and you can't celebrate what you never track.

This is your reminder that wealth doesn't just show up, it responds to structure. Every line you check, every category you review, every update you make is a love letter to your future self. Many think of financial freedom as one big win. In reality, it's a collection of small, consistent checkmarks that build the life you prayed for.

Say it with me:

- "I check-in because I care."
- "I manage because I matter."
- "My progress deserves my attention."
- "Organization is my superpower."

Affirm this truth: "I am the CFO of my life. I manage with wisdom. I spend with intention. I save with strategy. I give with grace. My checklist isn't pressure, it's peace. Every step I take is proof that I am becoming the woman who not only earns well but manages well, loves well, and leads her legacy with confidence."

Now, before you close this book, grab a pen and your courage. Do your first full purse check. Face it, fix it, and free yourself. The only thing standing between the life you dream of and the one you're living...is the checklist you have yet to complete.

Quick Exercise: Purse Check Audit

Once a quarter, answer the following questions.

What financial wins am I most proud of since my last check-in?

_____

_____

_____

_____

_____

_____

What's one leak I need to plug this month (subscription, spending habit, delay)?

_____

_____

_____

_____

_____

Which part of my checklist gives me the most anxiety, and why?

_____

_____

_____

_____

_____

What can I automate to make progress easier?

_____

_____

_____

_____

_____

What's one new goal I can add to next quarter's list?

_____

_____

_____

_____

_____

_____

Bonus Challenge: Create a "money Monday" ritual.

Spend 30 minutes at the start of each week reviewing your budget, bills, payments, and savings. Light a candle, play some music, make it sacred. Consistency turns chaos into confidence.

www.ingramcontent.com/pod-product-compliance
Lightning Source LLC
Chambersburg PA
CBHW040859210326
41597CB00029B/4903